# NINE PORTRAITS OF JESUS

## Discovering Jesus
## through the *Enneagram*

by
Robert J. Nogosek, C.S.C.

Dimension Books, Inc.
Denville, New Jersey 07834

ISBN 0-87193-260-1

# TABLE OF CONTENTS

## AUTHOR'S FOREWORD

I was introduced to the spirituality of the Enneagram by a series of workshops given by Father Pat O'Leary, S.J., and Sister Maria Beesing, O.P., from the Jesuit Retreat House in Cleveland, Ohio. During the first of those workshops, which was given in 1981 at the Benedictine Center at Beech Grove, Indiana, a remark by Father Pat enkindled my interest in discovering Jesus through the Enneagram. This remark was that since the Enneagram is based on the distinction of sin types, Jesus would have all nine personality types because he was without sin. Immediately I resolved to study the gospels from the perspective of the Enneagram to see if there was evidence for this.

The first result of my study was published privately in 1983 by the Benedictine Center at Beech Grove, Indiana, as a study guide for small group dialogue, and was entitled "Reflections on Gospel Values." Substantially the same material became Chapter 2, "The Enneagramic Jesus", in *The Enneagram: A Journey of Self Discovery,* which I co-authored with Patrick H. O'Leary, S.J., and Maria Beesing, O.P., and was published by Dimension Books, Inc., in 1984.

In the meantime I had been busy using the material in a preached retreat entitled "Nine Portraits of Jesus." Through this experience of preaching and personal interaction with hundreds of retreatants, I grew in appreciation of the value of applying the Enneagram to Jesus. Through the encouragement of Tom Coffey, Editor of Dimension Books, it was decided to publish the talks of this retreat as a book.

Since this book is the result of a preached retreat, it consists in a series of meditations on the spirituality of the Enneagram. At the end of each chapter I have added some scripture references for private meditation and also three questions for small group dialogue. At the end of the book I have included a format for using this material in a small group, which would meet every two or three weeks for personal and spiritual growth.

I owe a special word of gratitude to Suzanne Brown, Sr. Anton Marie Voissem, S.S.N.D., and Dr. J. Massyngbaerde Ford, each of whom carefully went over the manuscript and offered suggestions to make the work more attractive.

# DISCOVERING JESUS
# THROUGH THE ENNEAGRAM

It has always been a great marvel to christians that the Son of God could have become a man living in this world and at a time within recorded history. When walking about the country in which he lived, we can see not only the mountains and bodies of water he saw, but also some of the roadways, and even the same stones. Yet he created the universe long before, at the side of his Father in the one life they enjoy in their divine Spirit. When we consider the billions of galaxies now visible to human wonder, arranged as they are in great clusters, it startles us that their Creator could reveal himself personally as Jesus, and that he indeed did so. Although we can reach out to those clusters of galaxies through our scientific instruments and seek to discover the natural laws governing their arrangement and development, we experience an awe much greater in discovering that their Lawmaker is so much interested in us that he became a human being. As Jesus said, we are all gods (Jn 10:34f), for our God is our everlasting Friend, and we walk down a road with him as adopted children of his Father.

Considerations such as these, however, became an obstacle in taking a close look at the inner personality of Jesus according to his feelings, attitudes and motives. Great theologians, such as St. Thomas of Aquinas, assumed that the human experience of Jesus while he walked this earth had to be very different from ours because of what was called "the hypostatic union". Theology used words and phrases like "incarnation," "assuming a human nature," and "one divine person in two natures," all of which set Jesus apart from our own embodied experience of life. St. Thomas even concluded that Jesus enjoyed the direct sight of God in his human soul as he walked the earth, an experience which is the basic cause of the eternal joy of heaven.[1]

In our time theologians have tried to take another look at such teachings, and have decided that the enfleshment, or incarnation, means that Jesus must have experienced his inner human life as we do. Rather than reading his divinity "into" his humanness, we should read his divinity "off of" his humanness. Instead of taking the abstractions we have to describe God, such as all-knowing and all-perfect, and then deducing that this has to be true of Jesus, we should study what God is like from the way Jesus acts.

To know God, then, involves knowing the human character of Jesus. In Jesus above all, humanity is the image and likeness of God. He did not come wearing his humanness like some clothes put on, but rather he brought the essence of being human to its full capacity of revealing what God is like.

That essence itself becomes known through what we call *personality.* God is not revealed mainly by

---

[1]*Summa Theologiae,* IIIa, Q. 9, Art. 2.

Jesus' eyes and hands and legs, and all the other visible parts of his human body, but rather by his inner feelings, understanding, virtues, and a multitude of other identifiable characteristics of attitude and behavior.

What we learn through Jesus is that God is a lot like us. We don't have his majesty, but the scriptures say that Jesus hid that through humility (Phil 2:6f). How else could he approach us as Friend without scaring the life out of us? Real warm and mutual love has to be based on persons being interdependent. By coming to know him as a person we can begin to love him as Friend, which is his own deep desire (cf Jn 15:15).

Jesus comes to us above all as *Savior,* and this involves something more than just knowing him and the revelation of God he brings to us. God's self-revelation is not identical with what we call his salvation. Revelation affects our perception, but salvation affects our whole being. While floundering in the water in fear of drowning, I may perceive a person on shore intending to risk her life to save me, but that knowledge does not in itself pull me out of the water. Similarly, to discover what God is like, especially knowing his love through the humanness of Jesus, is not enough to save us. We need to be rescued by his being in contact with us. That in principle was stated by early christian writers when they said that only that is saved in us which the Son of God assumed in his humanity.[1] In other words, we can only be saved to the extent that the way we are human is the way Jesus

[1]St. John of Damascus (c. 675–749) stated: "Had there been anything of me not assumed, it would not have been saved" (*Orthodox Faith,* bk 2, lect. 1).

is human. He has to have what we have in order to save it in us.

I submit that the study of the enneagram personality theory elucidates in a new way what Jesus assumed in his human nature, and thus saved in us. The enneagram system demonstrates that there are nine ways of expressing what it is to be human. Since Jesus came to save all of us by becoming as we are, each of us should be able to discover in him our own way of being human.

At once, however, we come to up against the fact that all nine types in the enneagram are "sin types," built up due to a defense mechanism we have chosen to defend a compulsion special to us. In our Christian teaching we are accustomed to say that Jesus was sinless first of all in the sense of no wrongdoing, as is recorded in his statement: "Who can convict me of sin?" (Jn 8:46) Through theological reflection Christians have also concluded that Jesus was free of original sin, and hence also of what theology calls "concupiscence," which is a tendency to sin we discover in our nature. Granted then, that Jesus had no actual sin and no concupiscence, in enneagram language he would have had no compulsions. Since the types are differentiated by the specific compulsions, we conclude that his personality spontaneously expressed ALL NINE TYPES. Each type is a specific way of being human. All nine together are the perfect expression of humanness. Jesus could be that fully human being. Indeed, he was *the first to be fully human.*

*Method and Purpose of this Study*

It is one thing, however, to *theorize* that Jesus' personality expressed all nine types, and quite another to *demonstrate* that this is the way Jesus was experienced as a person by others who knew him. To make this "demonstration", I have looked at each enneagram type in succession and asked three questions of each:

1. How does Jesus express the gifts of this type?

2. What is the compulsion, or "trap", of this type, which, as sinless, Jesus would have avoided?

3. How did he, in fact, avoid that compulsion? (Here I have looked for leads into his motivation, and also noted his teaching, assuming that his teaching came from the way he already lived.)

For me this method of inquiry has been immensely fruitful. Not only has it increased my *affective knowledge* of the Lord as presented in the gospels, but it has also given me a much greater appreciation of the *giftedness* of each of the nine types.

I had been concerned about what effect the basic *negativity* of the enneagram system was having on some people. One of my Holy Cross friends told me that finding out his enneagram type was very discouraging for him, "because" as he said, "you come to realize you are stuck with it". In effect, once a FIVE, always a FIVE,—and he was a FIVE, as I also am. One can hope one's NUMBER is no longer "compulsed" but "redeemed", but we still know the compulsion is always *there.* I may end up saying, "I wish I were not as I am," which contradicts the healthy self-esteem we are called to have as sons and daughters of divine adoption. We are, after all, loved by God just as we

are. I need to experience this by being convinced
that I am basically a good and lovable person who is
cherished by God. Theologically we state this by
saying we are chosen and graced in our personal
being. Once I know, however, that Jesus in his personality really did express *my type,* I will feel a lot better
about being this type myself, despite its negative
connotations. In addition, this helps me acquire an
insight into how *I* am to be his *disciple* by trying to
live out my own NUMBER the way he did. By seeing
precisely where Jesus in his own attitudes overcame
or avoided the trap of my enneagram type I can come
to see how the message of the gospel particularly
applies to my own salvation. It also implies that by
expressing humanness through one of the enneagram
types I am by that very fact reflecting the personality
of Jesus himself.

Throughout these meditations on Jesus we will
leave aside as much as possible the terms of the
enneagram system and seek to see Jesus with the
inner light of contemplation focused directly on the
gospels themselves. Not only will this be a help for
those readers who do not share our excitement about
the enneagram, but it also will be more faithful to the
sources we have available for our investigation. Like
these sources, let us begin not with Jesus as an adult,
but with the background of his family and home life.
Subsequently we will undertake an "enneagramic"
knowledge of Jesus according to what we have called
his NINE PORTRAITS.

## THE ENNEAGRAM: A Call to Conversion

One early use of the insights of the Enneagram personality types was in a course on prayer given by Fr. Tad Dunne, S.J., at Creighton University, Omaha, Nebraska, in the summer of 1980.[1] During a session on the prayer of repentance he placed around the room placards, each bearing the names of a capital sin derived from the Enneagram, and then told the students to stand under the name of their "favorite sin". No one was exempt from choosing one of the sins. It was amusing for the students under each placard to look at one another and say: "Oh, yours is also LUST (or GLUTTONY, PRIDE, ENVY, etc.)!"

That is the way it is with the Enneagram personality theory. We all have to fit in somewhere as having a predominant fault, and as a consequence, to embark on an Enneagram study which challenges us to *conversion*. At the same time the Enneagram analysis of the personality uncovers a formidable hindrance in ourselves, namely, that we have taken our predominant fault and made it willy-nilly into what we consider to be our predominant virtue.[2] This makes repentance and conversion practically impossible until we discover our myopia concerning what we consider to be our personal fulfillment. Characteristically, we have looked at our fulfillment as something we can attain by ourselves, and in order to control our lives have limited for ourselves what we can be as a human personality. This

[1]Some of his material is included in *THE ENNEAGRAM: A Journey of Self Discovery,* by Maria Beesing, O.P., Robert J. Nogosek, C.S.C., & Patrick H. O'Leary, S.J., Dimension Books, Denville, N.J., 1984, pp. 100–114.
[2] *Ibid.,* p. 110.

myopia is expressed as our preferred PRIDE, which is better expressed by the word "hubris" (See diagram, p. 132) This hubris, or overweening pride, is a blindness, for it exists in our shadow. In our study of how Jesus expressed each of the enneagram types, we will especially seek to see not only the absence of this shadow in him, but also how his gospel can bring light and healing to the shadow that remains in us.

The nine sin types can conveniently be placed in three groups, depending on how they each limit their fulfillment to how they are as persons, to adjusting to the world, and to changing the environment.[1]

### Limiting Goodness to How I Am

Some personality types limit their goodness to *how they are as persons.* This is true for the EIGHT, TWO, and FIVE.

EIGHTS take too much pride on *being strong.* They think their goodness comes mainly from being assertive. As a consequence, they lack remorse when they intimidate others, step on the turf of others, or habitually tell others what to do. EIGHTS make the mistake of thinking tenderness is weakness, and they fail to see that *giving in* could be an expression of love.

TWOS take too much pride in *being needed.* In doing so, they don't notice how they try to make others dependent on them,—something which is quite selfish. They fail to see that to let others serve them would be an expression of humility.

FIVES take too much pride in *being wise* and not

---

[1]Ibid., pp. 110-114.

stupid. They are always thinking things out for themselves, which causes them to be aloof from others, and observers rather than participants in life. By seeking to control their time and schedule in order to carry out their projects of study, they fail to see their fault in avoiding involvement with others.

## Limiting Goodness to Conformity

Other personality types limit their goodness too much to *adjusting to the world as it is.* This is true for the THREE, NINE, and SIX.

THREES take too much pride in *being successful.* Since success is really the result of what others think of them, success becomes a matter of vainglory, subject to what others respond to and praise. THREES tend to think their worth depends on their own success, and hence they may make use of others to that end. They fail to see that the virtue of humility often is best realized through the experience of humiliations coming out of failure in the eyes of others.

NINES make a god of *being easy-going.* They tend to make life a routine, and draw back from whatever will disrupt their own peace. They tend to belittle those who are trying to change the world, and fail to take to heart the call they receive from God to become active in making the world better.

SIXES limit their goodness too much to *being obedient.* They think all virtue is obedience, rather than commitment to values. Since they already experience life as full of demands on them, they avoid acquiring new knowledge, because it would only serve to enlarge their responsibilities. SIXES have a great tendency to self-righteousness, i.e., being proud that they never commit sin. They often limit sin to the breaking of laws, and fail to deal with what can be a great cause of sin, namely, their own inner fears.

## Limiting Goodness to Changing the Environment

The three other personality types limit their goodness too much to what is outside themselves, especially to *what they can change in their environment.* This is true for the ONE, SEVEN, and FOUR.

ONES are typically *dissatisfied with things as they are.* They think their criticism is a virtue, when actually it often would be more virtuous to accept the good that is already present in themselves and in others, rather than constantly looking at what is wrong.

SEVENS make a god of *being cheerful.* They don't want to notice pain in others, or even in themselves. They fail to see that it is authentic for a person to be serious or sad at times. In their craving for cheerfulness SEVENS take too lightly their lack of self-discipline and their excesses in the use of pleasures.

FOURS make a god of *being refined.* In their efforts to express their special feelings and good taste they tend to neglect the virtue of simplicity. They often go overboard in concern for their past sufferings, and fail to see that self-pity is a vice.

## PART TWO:
### Jesus . . .

## HIS MOTHER

The story of Jesus is preceded in scripture with the story of his young mother, Mary. In Luke's gospel her story begins with what she interpreted to be God's message to her through the Angel Gabriel:

Six months later the Angel Gabriel was sent from God to a city of Galilee named Nazareth, to a virgin who had been betrothed to a man whose name was Joseph, and the name of the virgin was Mary. On entering in he said to her: "Rejoice, O highly-favored-one, the Lord is with you!"

But she was greatly disturbed by this statement, and was trying to discern what sort of greeting this was.

Then the Angel said to her: "Don't be afraid, Mary, for you have learned of the favor you have before God. Behold, you will conceive in your womb and bear a son, and you will call his name Jesus. He will be great and will be called Son of the Most High, and the Lord God will give him the throne of David, his father, and he will reign over the house of Jacob forever, and there will be no end to his kingdom."

Then Mary said to the Angel: "How will this be, since I have not had sexual intercourse with a man?"

Then in answer the Angel said to her: "The Holy Spirit will come upon you, and the power of the Most High will over-shadow you; therefore the holy one being born will be called Son of God. Know also that your relative Elizabeth has conceived a son in her old age, and this is the sixth month with her who was called the barren one, because anything is possible with God.

Then Mary said: "You are looking at the slave of the Lord. let it be done to me according to your word."

The Angel then left her.

This message came to her while at home with her parents in Galilee at the town of Nazareth, which is north of Jerusalem at a distance requiring a journey of four or five days. According to the Aprocryphal Gospels in early christian tradition Mary had lived at the Temple in Jerusalem, which was an educational as well as a worship institution. The fact that her cousin Elizabeth was married to a Jewish priest who served in the Temple encourages us to believe this. Such opportunity for learning would have enabled her to be able to read the scriptures and know them well.

If such be the case, we can imagine Mary as familiar with both the country and the city. She would have been accustomed already at a young age to travel between Nazareth and Jerusalem. We would think of her not as a shy Jewish girl hiding behind her shawl, but as a young person able to meet people and to communicate readily with them. Although her home town was the hamlet of Nazareth and occupied an area no greater than four modern city blocks each way, Mary's horizons as a young girl already would have been stretched much beyond that.

We may suppose that the man Joseph came into her life after she had finished school and returned to Nazareth. Her parents would have arranged the betrothal, even though she may have hardly known him herself. He would have been picked out because of his religious faithfulness and his ability to support a wife. It is likely he was somewhat older than she, as christians traditionally have imagined, for it would take some maturity to become the town carpenter and inherit a carpenter shop from his father or another relative.

The carpenter trade would mainly have served

farmers, for homes were made of stone and the poor people of Nazareth would have little furniture. Farm implements were made of wood, and farmers would have a lot of need for repair work. For this reason, his carpenter shop in the center of town would be similar in purpose to a blacksmith shop in early America. Farmers would have urgent repairs to be done and the hours of work would be from dawn to dusk. Not much income would be coming in, for farmers are always in debt, and they would be asking for credit until after the next harvest. The carpenter shop would be a lively place to be, where news was exchanged and people found out about the needs of one another.

We get the impression Joseph was a quiet man. The evangelists do not record even one word he said. He was very sensitive to God's Providence, and like Mary considered himself to be on this earth to serve God.

For her part, Mary accepted her parents' arrangements for her betrothal to Joseph, as would be expected of her by tradition. Concerning all this, however, she could have been somewhat uneasy and may have been praying about it over scripture when she received God's great message from the angel.

*The Annunciation*

Mary was dumbfounded by the angel's greeting, for in place of her name, Mary, he gave her an exalted title which indicated she was someone the angel would bow before in reverence. According to the title she was highly favored by God, or, as it has often been interpreted, she was "full of grace". It was the title rather than the angel that frightened her, but he tried to get her to relax and be joyful at hearing his message which he said came from God.

Being used to long hours of meditation over God's word, she tried to associate this message with the language of the scriptures. The angel immediately aided her in this by referring to the prophetic passage of Isaiah 7:14, which proclaimed that as a special sign a virgin would conceive, bear a son, and name him Emmanuel, a name meaning "God-is-with-us." Instead of saying Emmanuel the angel gave the name Jesus, which in Hebrew means "God-saves," and in place of "virgin" he used her name. This implied that it was while remaining a virgin that she was to conceive, bear a son, and at his circumcision name him Jesus. The evangelist Matthew takes pains to insist that she fulfilled this sign by not having intercourse with Joseph before Jesus was born (Mt 1:25).

In her actual dialogue with the angel Mary seems to have understood that her son was to be conceived right at that moment. This could explain her objection about not having knowledge of a man by sexual intercourse. Her question, then, was how could she conceive right at this moment. The angel's response satisfied her: it would be by the power of God's Holy Spirit. She then offered herself completely to God as his slave, knowing that in some sense her presence would bring God's grace to others.

We may be sure that as soon as possible she took Joseph aside and communicated to him all that had happened to her. It was his right to know not only that she was pregnant, but how and why. Such explanations could come only through her. It would not be right for her to keep this as her "little secret". Anyway, no girl can be only a "little bit" pregnant. They were betrothed, which in Jewish custom actually gave them the right to marital intercourse, even though the actual marriage would begin when she was brought to live with him in his house.

This is why Joseph thought of a divorce. Surely these thoughts of his came as a shock to Mary, for couldn't she expect that Joseph, her betrothed, would believe her story of the angel? What Mary had to do was to wait for him to catch up with her spiritually. The only way he would ever be able to be truly united with her in his heart would be that he, too, would have his own personal knowledge of God's action with her. This he received, as he later said, by an angel speaking to him in a dream, with a message identical to that which Mary shared with him (Mt 1:20ff). He was also told not to fear to take her into his house as his wife. It was fortunate for Mary that Joseph took his dreams seriously, just as his namesake in the Book of Genesis had done in patriarchal times.

Joseph followed these instructions, even though this probably meant announcing their marriage earlier than others would have expected. As soon as she came into his house with her belongings, however, he found her packing her travelling bag, and off she went alone to visit her relative Elizabeth. Although christians have thought of her simply going out to help her aged cousin in the difficulties of bringing forth a child for the first time, the main reason may have been that Mary knew she and Joseph were not to have sexual intercourse and it was best to avoid the possibility of this as they began their marriage.

Being separated from each other for a while could help both of them follow better the instincts God would give them on how to live as husband and wife. This would have its repercussions for Joseph as he continued working in his carpenter shop in Nazareth. Even good people could be very unkind with their gossip and off-color jokes about his bride's sudden departure. Joseph had wanted to avoid Mary's suffering shame when he had first learned of her pregnancy, and for that reason had thought of a quiet divorce. Now her departure brought shame to him in this little town. Right after the very public act of taking his bride into his house, everyone could see she had packed her bags and gone off alone without much of an explanation.

### The Visit to Elizabeth (Lk 1:39-56)

We are told that Mary went up to the mountain area in haste, as though led by the Holy Spirit. The ordinariness of the trip was climaxed by another revelatory moment as she walked into the summer cottage where Elizabeth was in seclusion at Ain Karin. Mary burst into the house with a happy greeting. In that very greeting Elizabeth felt Mary's presence bringing the grace of God to her and to the child she was to bear in a few months. Mary, in turn, sensed being affirmed by God through the words of Elizabeth, who said she was blessed among all women who ever would live, and was worthy of praise especially because of her faith in God's word to her.

Mary herself was also moved in the Spirit and said she saw that the humiliation of her pregnancy outside marriage was a means for God to bless the whole human race. Through her pregnancy God was sending salvation to other poor persons like herself. She saw that for generations to come the poor and afflicted would be lifted up and comforted by God, whereas the wealthy and powerful of this world would be brought down from their exalted positions in society. As a young and pregnant bride Mary was excited about what her life could do for others. She saw her own humiliation and powerlessness as a means God would use to bring peace, justice, and joy to the whole human family, not only in her time, but for all future ages.

After Elizabeth's child was born, Mary hurried home. Her heart yearned to be there with Joseph. It had been his home; now it was hers also.

*The Birth of Jesus (Lk 2:1-20)*

The narrative of Jesus' birth in Luke's gospel centers on Mary, and does not describe Joseph's feelings. Mary seems very much alone, trusting in God, meditating on events, and obeying her husband, who had insisted they must go to register at Bethlehem just as her child was due. The picture we get is that Mary brought forth her son alone, and herself wrapped the baby in winding cloths. The cave serving as their shelter that night served as a barn for animals. It was cold, damp, and smelly. They had little or no money. The people who came were themselves simply poor shepherds, without any education and even without clean clothes. They said they had received the joyous message they had received from angels to look for the savior as a baby lying in a manger. Their coming was another revelatory event Mary would keep in her heart for meditation, but it did not make the cave smell any better or keep out the cold.

## The Presentation in the Temple (Lk 2:22-39)

The Holy Family remained in Bethlehem for some time after the birth of Jesus. Probably they found lodging with relatives, with whom they celebrated the circumcision the following week. A month later they took their child to the Temple in Jerusalem, which was not many miles distant from Bethlehem.

We can imagine Mary and Joseph going to Jerusalem that day with great joy. Mary would be thrilled at caring for her baby, holding him and nursing him on the way. After they arrived in the great city, they were about to enter the Temple area when a man named Simeon surprised them. We are told he had received a word from God to go from his house to the Temple in order to see the one promised in the scriptures to bring salvation to all nations through Israel. It was another *kairos,* or revelatory moment, for Mary and Joseph, breaking into what was otherwise ordinary daily life. Like us they were learning to be open to the surprises of God's intervening action while at the same time trying to do what was best in their decisions and to go on with their life as ordinary human beings.

## PASSAGES FOR MEDITATION

The Annunciation—Luke 1:26-38.
Joseph's Reaction—Matthew 1:18-25.
The Visit to Elizabeth—Luke 1:39-56.
The Birth of Jesus—Luke 2:1-21.
The Presentation in the Temple—Luke 2:22-38.

## QUESTIONS FOR DIALOGUE

1. In what way is Mary an example to us in offering herself to God as his disciple?
2. How have our own humiliations and even shame before others been used by God to bring us closer to him and to benefit others?
3. How do we experience christian life on two levels: that of ordinary human experience and that of God's actions and interventions?

## HIS HOME LIFE

Among the evangelists, St. Luke in particular invites us to study the development of Jesus' character beginning with his years of childhood. He gives us a glimpse of the interaction of Jesus with his parents in the story of the loss at Jerusalem when Jesus was twelve:

> And his parents went year by year to Jerusalem at the feast of Passover. And when he became twelve years old they went there according to the custom of the feast, and afterwards, on their return, the boy Jesus remained in Jerusalem without his parents knowing it. Supposing, however, that he was with the group, they went a day's journey and looked for him among their relatives and acquaintances; and when they did not find him they returned to Jerusalem to look for him. Then it happened that after three days they found him in the temple sitting among the teachers, listening to them and questioning them. And all who heard him were amazed at his intelligence and his answers. And when his parents saw him they were astonished and his mother said to him: "Child, why did you do this to us? See how your father and I have been greatly distressed looking for you." Then he said to them: "Why did you seek me? Did you not know that I had to be about the concerns of my Father?" But they did not understand the word he spoke to them. Then he went down with them and came to Nazareth, and was subject to them. And his mother carefully kept all these matters in her heart. And Jesus grew in wisdom and age and grace before God and humankind.
>
> (Luke 2:41–52)

This is the first portrait we are given in the scriptures of the personality of Jesus. He is twelve. The story indicates that his parents considered him very able to be on his own. Each year for Passover they had been accustomed as a family to join other pilgrims from Nazareth and surrounding towns for the journey of four or five days to Jerusalem.

On this occasion, after the holy days were over,

Mary and Joseph started back for home. Probably they were in separate caravans; in any case, the fact that Jesus was not walking with them did not cause them concern. They assumed he would be with their relatives, or with his young friends. They had made this journey many times with him before. Now that he was old enough for what we call today the bar mitzvah, they were accustomed to his doing things on his own.

It came, then, as a great surprise as they camped for the first night to discover he was nowhere to be found among any of those who had accompanied them on pilgrimage from Nazareth. He had not given them any indication that he would stay behind. They were used to his being obedient and responsible to them. Their immediate thought was that something tragic had happened to him.

Hurrying back to Jerusalem, they searched for him, but it was not until the third day that they came upon him in the Temple. Obviously that was not the first place where they looked. There he was in the midst of the teachers at the Temple. He was acting just like one of the rabbinical students, answering questions and in turn asking questions of the teachers. As they entered they saw him actually at the center of attention because of his brilliant questions and answers. Here he was, a boy from the country with little formal schooling and a Galilean accent, displaying such a probing mind and forceful personality.

Obviously, during the holy days Jesus had discovered something new in his life. In the course of the religious ceremonies his Father had spoken to his little boy heart in a new way, and Jesus wanted to stay where this had happened in order to understand more. He had a deep yearning to know the scriptures and all they said about the coming Kingdom of God. Most likely he had met some other young men who were students at the Temple and they had persuaded him to stay with them and to listen to their teachers.

Jesus would have liked to have had the opportunity for a good education in the scriptures and in the Hebrew traditions. Perhaps he thought that when his parents saw this deep desire of his, they would allow him to stay at the Temple. His mother, however, did not respond in that way. She told him to come home.

Jesus' words to his mother about the concerns of his Father suggest that Jesus knew not only that God was his Father, but also that he had a mission to fulfill God's Plan for the world. Wouldn't he need a good theological education to be able to know the promises of God that he was to fulfill? His mother, however, did not look at it this way. She did not even give it a consideration. It wasn't that she disbelieved in Jesus' mission. She had been the first to report it, at least to her immediate family. She knew Jesus was to bring salvation to the whole world, but as her Magnificat indicates, it would be especially to the poor that he would proclaim the news of God's Kingdom. He needed to grow up with the poor and ordinary people of Nazareth, not be couped up in a boarding school and spend his youth memorizing rabbinical traditions.

Jesus had heard his Father speak to him a new word during the religious ceremonies. Now, however, he heard his Father speaking to him in another way, namely, through his parents. Jesus was being told he was not to grow up in an exclusive Hebrew school, but was to go back to live with his parents and to prepare for his life mission by growing up in Nazareth. He had discovered the thrill of unrolling the Hebrew scrolls and having great scholars interpret the meaning of each sacred word. He was to give this up, however, just as there were many other good things he would have to leave aside in his life out of obedience to the way of life designed for him by the Father.

With the wisdom of her parental heart, Mary knew that the way Jesus grew up was very important to the fulfillment of God's plans for him. She saw that an elite Hebrew school was not the right place for that. It was Joseph's decision, too, that Jesus was to follow Joseph by becoming an artisan. What Jesus needed was to belong to the people of his small town and to discover God in family life. This would give him the best environment for his social and sexual development. He needed to learn how to love life and to love people as they were, especially poor people. Growing up in Nazareth with his relatives and townspeople would teach him how to relate and interact with the kind of people he was to serve and save. Mary had seen enough of the rigidity of those who were the acknowledged experts in religious teaching. Those professional rabbinical schools in Jerusalem produced legalistic men who lacked sensitivity to the human heart and really knew very little about life, or even about God.

There in his home town Jesus grew in wisdom, stature and favor before God and others (Lk 2:52). Life itself was his school. This itself would be the message of the coming of God's Kingdom, — that the Kingdom would come in the ordinary events of life. It did mean, though, that Jesus would also remain a man who had had very little schooling. In teaching others he would have to do the best he could in communicating what he had learned from his life experience and from meditating on scripture. The Father wanted his divine Son to empty himself not only by becoming human and mortal (Ph 2:7), but also by being a man with little formal education. His own experience of life would be like that of the "lowly" he had come to exalt (Lk 1:52).

## Learning from His Mother

Mary, for her part, could continue being a prayer companion for her Son. Jesus surely appreciated his mother's deep knowledge of the scriptures and her sharing with him the fruit of her meditation on God's word. We see in Mary's personality the characteristic of waiting for God to take the initiative. Like the Woman of the Apocalypse, she seems always "pregnant" (Rev 12:4), always in waiting for the coming of God into the world. This combined attitude of waiting for God and expecting great events of God acting in history penetrated the atmosphere of the home Mary created with Joseph and Jesus. She thereby helped her Son become involved with life as it presented itself in Nazareth and to be sensitive to whatever happened. They waited for God to call. The Messiah was to be God's agent in the transformation of history. It was up to the Author of that saving work to decide when and how to call forth his chosen one. In the meantime, besides giving Jesus a home where he could share himself as he waited, Mary gave him her own company and companionship.

From both Mary and Joseph Jesus learned how to reflect in a religious way on the many small details of life. As a youngster Jesus saw the wonder of many ordinary things. There was, for example, the wonder of yeast as his mother made bread. He noticed how she kneaded a small bit of yeast into the dough. Then in just a few hours what had been a heavy and even bitter-tasting mass would rise and be transformed into something sweet and light. Later on in his preaching, Jesus would say that this was like the way God would transform the world. His followers as a community of faith and love would be mixed in with the world, like yeast is mixed with dough (Mt 13:33), and thereby the whole world would become God's Kingdom. This meditation from Jesus' boyhood continues to challenge us whenever we read it. We are to question ourselves on whether we actually are transforming our society today. If not, it could be because we are too separate from the world,—not "kneaded in",—or because we are too much like the world,— just part of the dough rather than being like yeast.

Another possible event in his mother's life Jesus may have meditated on was how she reacted when a silver coin fell off her wedding cap and rolled out of sight. She lit an oil lamp in order to see better, since their home was mainly a cave in the hill and was without much in the way of windows. She got a broom, swept the floor, and took the lamp to look under the bed. Her face had an anxious expression. She prayed out loud that the Father would help them. Then suddenly she found it! She ran to the neighbors and said they had to celebrate because God had helped her find the lost coin (Lk 15:8-10).

The story acquaints us with the poverty of Jesus' home. For Jesus, however, it later conveyed a message of the good news of God's Kingdom. He said that anyone of his followers that drops away from union with God is like that drachma which was lost. Although to others such a person may not seem important, to God this represents a great loss, and like the woman in the story God will search and search for ways to bring that person back into communion with him. When that happens,—that is, when the person repents,—God's house is filled with delight. As Jesus said, "there is great rejoicing among the angels of God".

As is typical of little boys, Jesus would wear holes in his robe from crawling on the ground or tear it while climbing trees. To mend the hole or tear his mother would cut out a patch from a discarded robe of Joseph's. Jesus perhaps asked his mother why she did not use new cloth for the patch. She explained that although his robe would no longer shrink when she washed it, the patch of new cloth would do so, and that would ruin the mending by pulling out the threads. Since Joseph's old robe had already been washed many times, its cloth would not shrink any more. Later on, in preaching the gospel, Jesus said to his fellow Jews that his new message could not be used just as a patch on their traditional way of living their religion (Mt 9:16). That would be like putting a new patch on old clothes. It just would not last. Instead, to respond to his religious message they had to take on a whole new way of life. The gospel life cannot just be an addition or revision of their Jewish traditions. Out of that came, then, the whole new freedom of christians from the Jewish law that we particularly give credit to St. Paul for announcing (Gal 5:1).

## Learning from Joseph

Joseph also had a lot to teach the young Jesus. In particular, as a skilled artisan, he taught Jesus to labor with his hands and to appreciate the nobility of work. To be a good carpenter involves careful attention to details. Custom service can be given to others because of the skills one has developed and used. The nobility of work was deeply engrained in the Hebrew culture, as is evidenced especially by the creation stories in Genesis, where God set the example of going to work during the week and then resting on the seventh day. Man and woman were then placed on earth to tend and develop by their work what God had created by his work. Later on the message that God is at work would be very important in Jesus' preaching. Jesus saw his whole life as doing the work of God, who intended to bring about his Kingdom through human history.

Joseph was self-employed, and through learning the skills of a carpenter Jesus himself later succeeded Joseph in running the shop. This moulded his character in responsibility, self-discipline, and appreciation of his own talents and those of others. Many of Jesus' later disciples would also be self-employed men. This probably gave them a greater openness to learning new things, as well as the ability to take off from work to spend time with Jesus. As for Jesus himself, he would move from running his own carpenter shop to organizing his own religious movement. He knew what it was to be a good boss. He also learned through the daily work at the carpenter shop what it meant to work all day long, be available to those who needed urgent repairs, and to live without much income. His public life shows that kind of discipline, patience, and spirit of service.

Jesus took a great interest in the life of the farmers who came to his shop. He became acquainted with what farm work was like. We can imagine him as a young man asking a farmer to let him try plowing. As he started out grasping the reins and holding the handles of the plow at the same time with his strong arms, he saw the furrows turn over, and then looked behind to see what he had accomplished. The farmer shouted to him to keep looking ahead. Sure enough, the moment he had taken his eye off what was ahead the plow had swerved from the straight furrow he was supposed to be making. Later on, Jesus used such an experience to tell his followers that to live his gospel they had to keep looking ahead. As he said: "Anyone who starts to plow and then keeps looking back is of no use for the Kingdom of God" (Lk 9:62). In other words, we have to let God lead us into a new future, and not keep trying to hold on to what we had in the past.

Jesus' experience with farmers led him to use many parables based on agriculture in his preaching. Most famous is that of the sower (Mt 13:4-9). Farmers recognized that many of the grains they sowed by broadcasting would not get rooted or for some other reason would not produce a crop, but enough would get planted to fill the field with ripe heads of wheat for the harvest. Jesus saw this as first of all a message to himself as a preacher. To proclaim God's message of the Kingdom would not convert everyone who heard him. Only some would take the message to heart, but there would be some. Every heralder of the gospel needs to take this into account and avoid getting over-confident at the beginning and over-discouraged with the end results in evangelization.

Another parable on raising crops concerned the weeds that grew up in the field. As Jesus pointed out, the farmer cannot do much about the weeds once they are there, not even when they are just coming up. When the plants are small it is hard to distinguish weeds from grain, and in any case by going into the planted field to pull out the weeds the crop itself will be damaged. Farmers know that the way to deal with weeds is to prepare the ground well, and to avoid planting any weeds along with the wheat. Sometimes, though, someone with a grudge vandalizes the field by scattering weed seed in it (Mt 13:25). Jesus knew that religious leaders often were overly zealous in uprooting heresies and castigating persons for bad conduct. He wanted his own pastoral leaders to be more tolerant, and to leave the judgment and the sorting out of good and evil in the hands of God. In the end, at the harvest, God would sort out the weeds (Mt 13:30). The main job was to prepare the field and to do the planting. After that, you could count on the crop growing even at night while you were sleeping (Mk 4:27). We see the apostles following such attitudes in their early efforts in evangelizing, even among the pagans. They looked for the movement of grace in a person's heart. When they saw it, they were ready to baptize the person, and even his or her whole family, without the programs and paperwork normally associated today with bringing converts into the church (Cf Ac 16:14f, 29-34).

Farmers around Nazareth not only raised grain; they also tended vineyards. Jesus' preaching later reflected this also. The Old Testament, of course, already had a long tradition of identifying God's People with a vine God had planted on his land, and which God expected to produce an abundance of fruit for the good of other nations (cf Is 5:1ff). The main preparation for a good crop of grapes was pruning, or as Jesus called it, "cleansing" (Jn 15:2). In his preaching he identified himself as the new vine God has planted in the world, and his followers were the branches. Curiously enough, the image is not of a tree trunk out of which the branches spread, but of a vine, which consists only in branches. This conveys the message that the fruitfulness of Jesus' mission would be achieved by his followers through his life present in them. The pruning needed for the fruitfulness,—which on a vine is really an enormous cutting back,—would be accomplished in his followers by their accepting his word (Jn 15:3). Their lives would be pruned, or cleansed, by the sacrifices they would have to make to live out the gospel. Very little fruit is ever produced by vines which are not pruned.

It is in such ways as the preceding that Jesus was prepared for his public mission while living at Nazareth until he was about 30 years old. Such a background continually influenced the way he spoke and acted. It did not, however, fully explain the public figure he later became. As we shall later reflect on, when he left town to visit John the Baptist and then returned after his baptism, his townspeople hardly recognized him, and indeed no longer considered him as one of their own (Mt 13:53-57).

## PASSAGES FOR MEDITATION

Parables of the Kingdom—Matthew 13:1-52.
The Lost Silver Coin—Luke 15:8-10.
God's Work of Creating—Genesis 1:1-2:4.
The Vine and the Branches—John 15:1-17.

## QUESTIONS FOR DIALOGUE

1. How do I experience the presence of the Kingdom of God in ordinary events, such as in family life?
2. How does the gospel teach us to wait for God to take the initiative, while expecting that God will act in history?
3. How do I experience the nobility of work, especially from the fact that Jesus worked as a carpenter?

## PART THREE:
### ONE: His Discipline

ONES are *exacting* persons. They are hard on themselves and on others. All of us have had at least one teacher who insisted on *discipline* and our doing everything just right. At the time we may have hated her or him, but later on in life we probably are grateful that someone cared that much about our education, and drummed into us our grammar or our ability to do arithmetic. In such matters, as in most things in life, *details* and *being correct* may determine whether or not we will keep a job.

The gospels present Jesus as an exacting person. One such example is found in the Sermon on the Mount:

> Don't think that I came to destroy the law or the prophets. I did not come to destroy, but to fulfill. For truly I say to you, until earth and sky pass away, not one iota or one point of the law will pass away until everything comes to be. Therefore whoever breaks the least of these commandments and teaches it to others will be called least in the kingdom of heaven. But whoever obeys the least of the commandments and teaches others to do so will be called great in the kingdom of heaven. For I tell you that unless your rectitude exceeds that of the scribes and pharisees, you will not be able to enter the kingdom of heaven.
>
> (Mt 5:17-20)

Jesus had high expectations of his disciples. He taught them to be perfect in their observance of all the commandments. They were to be perfect in every way,—indeed much more "perfect" in their motives and behavior than the scribes and pharisees. They were always to be good, generous, honest and direct, fair towards others, and very responsible.

Whatever Jesus asked of his followers he first lived out himself. He put a lot of effort into expressing his ideals in his own conduct. He worked very hard at his ministry; in fact, his family thought he was working too hard and hurting his health. One day as he was engaged in teaching a group of people, his relatives sent word through the crowd that they wanted to see him, probably to tell him to take some time off for the sake of his health. When told his family members wanted to see him, Jesus' reaction was to say that those who listened to the word of God and lived it out constituted his family (Lk 8:21). He perhaps was being hard on his mother and relatives, but he was first of all being hard on himself.

ONES will readily identify with these characteristics of Jesus' personality. Like Jesus, they take pride in being hard-working and always ready to put in a great effort to do things well, especially in giving attention to details. Being very concerned to do what is right and avoid what is wrong, they expect a lot not only of others but also of themselves.

## Attention to Details as a Compulsion

In all this striving for correctness, however, ONES may fail to notice their shadow side, which develops precisely because they take such pride in doing good. In giving so much attention to perfection they cultivate an overly-critical attitude, and may be bothered by any imperfection they see. As ONES see it, things should be done right. *They* always try hard to do things right; others *should* do so also. If a ONE lives with persons who are overweight, he or she will keep noticing how they don't do anything about it. Of course, the ONE doesn't tell the others about it; *they* should know their fault of overeating and do something about it.

ONES are typically fussy about orderliness and cleanliness. After all, "there is a place for everything and everything should be in its place," and "cleanliness is next to godliness." Usually the ONE's mother is made the source of such imperatives. ONES usually are *dissatisfied* about something, and show this by an edginess in their voice. Their critical nature may cause others to be afraid of them. As a ONE, I may learn that my brother, who was a high school dropout, no longer writes to me. I once remarked to my sister about how poor his spelling is. It got back to him.

What ONES are most critical of, though, are themselves. They experience an inner critic that keeps telling them to check up on past behavior to see where they may have been wrong in something they did. ONES are much bothered by not getting things done the way they should be because there wasn't enough time. Whatever they do, they want to go over it again and do it better the next time. When ONES are told they have done something really well, they am still not satisfied, because they feel it could have been done better if they had had more time. ONES feel justified in being fussy and meticulous, because they see the details of how a thing is done as very important. Though they may not admit it, they can be stubborn in insisting that things be done their way. We have all heard the story of the man who married a schoolteacher. When he made love to her, if he did not do it right she made him do it over again.

This passion for perfection is a trap. It makes a person fussy, irritable, and always slightly on edge. The slighted imperfection seems to spoil the whole thing. Surely there is something wrong in such exaggerated exactitude.

*Jesus' Tolerance*

We can see that even though Jesus was an exacting teacher, he did not carry that over into being a fussy and meticulous person. Rather than picking people apart, he tended to accept them as they were. One example is the gospel story of the woman at the well (Jn 4:3-30). She came to the well in the heat of the day probably because other women in the town avoided her. She wasn't coming to be preached to; she just wanted to get her water and go home. She was a strong lady: she did not run away in tears when Jesus told her of her sinful life, but adroitly changed the subject. Jesus obviously enjoyed talking with her. He probably found it relaxing to talk with a woman after being on the road all day with his apostles. Despite her irregular marital situation, he did not chide her, but instead drew out of her a deep faith in the coming Messiah. As a result she became an apostle herself. She ran to the people of the town telling them about the man she met. She said he must be the Messiah, for he had told her all that she had ever done. We can imagine her going not only to the houses where the women were, but also into the bars to get the men to go out to meet Jesus. She had experienced Jesus' unconditional love. He had accepted and loved her just as she was. To do this, he not only broke through religious and cultural taboos in asking to drink from her bucket, but had shared himself with her on a very deep level. He invited her to drink from the deep well of his own person.

Another example of Jesus accepting a sinful woman is the story that took place at the house of Simon the Pharisee (Lk 7:36–50). Jesus was reclining there as a dinner guest when a woman from the street came in and stood at his feet. Tears welled from her eyes so abundantly that they fell on his feet. She let down her elegant hair to use to dry his feet, and then began kissing them. If the others in the room had not noticed her, they did when she opened an alabaster jar of imported perfume, which she poured on Jesus' feet.

There was dead silence, but Jesus could hear what the others were thinking: "If this man were the prophet, he would have known who and what sort of woman this is who is touching him . . . " What does Jesus do before all these he-men fishermen and religious leaders? He lets the woman express her love for him in the way she knows best. We are not told he was comfortable. He just accepted her as she was. He didn't tell her to go and get herself shaped up just right, or to see him privately. He made himself vulnerable by welcoming her love and repentance.

Before his host, Simon the Pharisee, Jesus pointed to the woman as a example of how we all should act. He said that her great love shows that much has been forgiven, and then said wryly that the person who doesn't love much hasn't had much forgiven. Despite all his moral exactitude, Jesus displayed not only tolerance toward others who have made moral mistakes, but even suggested that when there are few mistakes being made it could be that there isn't much love going on.

Another story that belongs in this context is that of the adulterous woman in John 8:1-11. This text seems to have been somewhat of a *scandal* to early christians, for it is absent from some early manuscripts of John's gospel. After all, the passage depicts Jesus expressing tolerance toward adultery.

At the time of this story, Jesus was commuting to Jerusalem each day from Bethany. It was about a week before his crucifixion. As he was standing and teaching in the midst a group of people in the temple area, some scribes and pharisees,—all men,—came up pushing a woman before them. They said they had caught her in the very act of committing adultery. They said that according to the "law of Moses" such a woman was to be stoned to death, and asked Jesus what he would say about it. Jesus knew they were trying to trap him. They were planning his arrest and wanted to get some evidence against him from his teaching. They knew it would be hard for him to say they should stone the woman because he was always insisting on compassion, but, on the other hand, if he contradicted an instruction of Moses this could be used against him as evidence of false teaching. Jesus, however, was not interested in having a theological debate. He was concerned about the woman, who stood there red-faced in shame. He saw her as his sister. She had done wrong, yes, but she did not

deserve to be exposed publicly in this way. Her
accusers did not care about her at all; they were just
*using* her to get at Jesus. Jesus himself shared the
embarrassment of the woman. He bent over and
began writing in the sand, as though doodling. He
probably sensed the inequality in such sanctions:
there was no such punishment for the *male* trans-
gressor. Straightening up, he said: "Let the one among
you who is sinless throw the first stone." Then he
stooped over and continued writing in the sand.
Gradually all the men left,—as the text says, "beginning
with the oldest,"—and Jesus was left alone with the
woman. Then he straightened up again and asked
her: "Woman, where are they? Didn't anyone condemn you?" She said: "No one, sir." Then Jesus said:
"Neither will I condemn you. From now on, though,
don't sin anymore."

Such stories of Jesus' compassion can be of great
help to the perfectionist personality of the ONE.
Tolerance and compassion are more important that
what is called "perfection." We notice that Jesus'
admonition to be "perfect as your heavenly Father is
perfect", as in Mt 5:48, is rendered by St Luke as:
"Be compassionate as your Father is compassionate"
(Lk 6:36). What Jesus is saying, even in Matthew's ver-
sion, is that we are to do good to all, just as God does
good not only to the just but to the unjust. God
actually shows a *tolerance* for evil and out of love he
affirms the good that is present in the midst of the bad.

In the Parable of the Weeds (Mt 13:24–30), we are
told that to enter the Kingdom of God, we need to
accept the weeds in our life along with the good seed.
To try to root out the weeds may result in uprooting

the good seed, perhaps especially because it would be so difficult to distinguish the weeds from the grain. What is important is to trust and affirm the good that is there. The good seed has power from within to grow and develop more good.

My "goodness" is not to be viewed according to some standard of perfection, but rather as a *power for growth.* I can learn from the Parable of the Weeds to focus on the good both in my life and in that of others. If it is accepted, trusted, and affirmed, this good, no matter how small, can develop into what Jesus portrayed as a good harvest. There is a power of God present both in nature and in grace that tends to enhance all that is already good. The law of the gospel, just as the law of nature, involves growth and development of the good already present, even though it be very small, as is the case of the mustard seed Mt 13:31f).

We are to give our attention, then, to the good that is already present, rather than to insist on "perfection." We can simply say, "That is where you are at now," not condoning the faults we see, but believing in the person's power to grow out of the present immaturity and imperfection. That is true first of all, of course, in how we view ourselves, for it is a psychological truth that we tend to project on others our own hidden judgment of ourselves.

For ONES a key paradox of the gospel is that we become perfect by accepting our imperfection. We need to acknowledge that the process of growth involves a lot of mistake-making, whether this be in how we express ourselves, how we learn a skill, or how we grow in the ability to love another. As Jesus suggested in the story of the woman in Simon's house, if we have made few mistakes in our lives it may be because we have not tried to love very much.

## PASSAGES FOR MEDITATION

Lessons on Tolerance—Matthew 5:38-48.
The Woman at the Well—John 4:1-42.
The Woman at the House of Simon the Pharisee—
  Luke 7:36-50.
The Adulterous Woman—John 8:1-11.

## QUESTIONS FOR DIALOGUE

1. When have we experienced in our lives too much stress on doing things perfectly or having everything very clean and orderly? What other values were being neglected?
2. How do we interpret "turning the other cheek" (Mt 5:39), and being tolerant towards injustice?
3. How do we see Jesus more concerned about growth than perfection?

## TWO: His Solicitude

One phrase that particularly captures the personality of Jesus is that he was "a man for others." He took pride in living to serve others, and taught his followers the same, as, for example, in the following passage:

> Then they came to Capernaum, and once they were in the house, Jesus asked them: "What were you discussing on the way?" But they were silent, for on the way they had been discussing who was the greatest. Then sitting down he called the twelve and said to them: "If anyone wants to be first, that person is to be the last of all and the servant of all. Then taking a child, he placed her in their midst. Then he put his arms around her, and said to them: "Whoever welcomes in my name a child like this welcomes me; and whoever welcomes me, welcomes not me but the One who sent me." (Mk 9:33-37)

TWOS take pride in being of service to others. Such an attitude was certainly of great value to Jesus. He insisted that he had come to serve, and not to be served (Mt 20:28). As he showed, serving others included hugs and other forms of warm hospitality, but it especially meant taking the initiative in helping others. This may mean coming to the rescue when another is embarrassed, or hurt, or simply left out. TWOS are great "rescuers", and so was Jesus.

We see Jesus being such a "rescuer" in the story of the wedding reception at Cana (Jn 2:1-11). The newly-married couple would be embarrassed that the wine had run out, and evidently they were too poor to provide more. Without being asked, Jesus rescued them from their embarrassment.

Another example, which is also at the beginning of

Jesus' public ministry, was his cure of Peter's mother-in-law (Mk 1:29–34). He had just moved from Nazareth to Capernaum. When he came back to Peter's home after being at the synagogue for sabbath worship, he was told that the mother-in-law of Peter was sick in bed with a fever. He went into her bedroom right away and, taking her by the hand, lifted her up out of bed. The fever left her immediately. She dressed and then served them a meal. Jesus did not wait to be asked to help; he simply cared for her need as soon as he was made aware of it.

## *The Obsession to be Helpful*

As rescuing persons, TWOS identify their personal WORTH with being of service to the needs of others. This can be so important that when there is nothing to do for another, they feel there is nothing to do at all. A spinoff from this will be their typical dislike for meetings. In their eyes, the only value of a meeting is the opportunity it gives for relating with people. The agendas of meetings, however, are not only for that purpose. As a consequence, during a meeting TWOS will busy themselves with ways of being of help to others, even if they find no better way than to open a window for fresh air or to serve coffee. This is why we see such persons knitting or writing letters during a meeting. At least in that way they feel they will be able to do something for somebody as the meeting goes on.

Because TWOS center their lives on being helpful to others they generally dislike self-analysis. They consider it wrong to focus their attention on themselves, and as regards others they do not want to analyze them but to help them. Their main interest is always in serving needs they find in others, especially in a "special" other.

These tendencies cover up a hidden spirit of independence and pride typically found in the rescuing personality. Although they may not recognize this, TWOS avoid being dependent on others. This comes from an attitude of denying that they themselves have any needs. They are the helpers; others are the helped. That is the way they want to relate to everybody, and especially to those whom they love. Such refusal to allow others to serve them is a baffling characteristic. Despite all their warmth, this hidden spirit of independence and pride makes them hard to relate to in an ongoing way, because they are always trying to put the persons they love in a situation of being served.

Here we have the makings of a serious compulsion: serving others with the intention of making them dependent. TWOS will want to find out your favorite food, or what dress you like best on them, so that they can relate to you by filling a "need" you have. Should you ask them about their favorite food, they will not answer, for they are not seeking to be served by you in any way. TWOS think this attitude of serving is selfless, but actually what they am trying to do is to *tie* others to themselves. This creates difficulties in a relationship when the other resists being made to feel dependent and simply does not want to relate in that way.

This sheds light on the story of an early visit of Jesus at the home of Mary and Martha at Bethany

(Lk 10:38–42). Martha was busy getting a meal ready, while her sister Mary was sitting at Jesus' feet. Probably all of this was taking place in the same room. Suddenly, Martha came over to where Jesus was sitting and complained to him: "Lord, don't you care that my sister has left me alone with the serving? Tell her then to come and help me." Jesus reacted by refusing to do that, and chided Martha for being anxious about many things. His statement suggested she was working too hard to prepare a lavish meal and that instead she should make the meal simple. As he said: "Only one thing is needed." Her sister, he said, had chosen the better part (or "portion"), and he was not going to take it away from her. Jesus was defending the right of a woman to sit at the feet of a rabbi to learn the word of God. Women should not think that all they can do is work in the kitchen. His main point, however, was that he had come to Martha's house to visit, and not to be served his favorite food. Jesus would have liked Martha also to have sat down with him to discuss the word of God. Instead of doing that, she was preoccupied with getting out a big meal in order to *do* something for him. This hindered her from experiencing the personal communion with Jesus that he desired.

TWOS usually are not drawn to spend much time alone in quiet prayer and reflection with the Lord. Such prayer, after all, is not *doing* anything, either for God or for others. It is doing something for themselves, but TWOS avoid paying attention to such private needs. They like to do things for God much more than simply commune with him.

What happens to TWOS when no one needs their

services? To reject their service is felt as a rejection of themselves, of all the worth that they think they have. The anger and feeling of rejection resulting from this can embitter them so much that they withdraw from others and harbor deep resentment against persons they once considered very special. They will always be angered when they feel unappreciated for their service. They think no one else is as able to serve the way they do, which is often true, because of the total preoccupation with which they go about doing it.

## The Meaning of Grace

It is especially at such times of feeling rejected that TWOS need to hear the gospel of God's grace. Grace concerns the revelation through Jesus of God's love for us. Already early in life, TWOS made a basic mistake in their approach to love. They came to think of love as something that can be *earned,* and they dedicated themselves to winning love by pleasing others. In this they confused love for what we call *appreciation.* This mistake hinders them from knowing real love,—the kind revealed by God in Jesus. That love is always experienced as *undeserved.*

What is meant by the term "grace" is that we have received an undeserved love from God. When I am loved by Jesus through another person's love what most strikes me,—and causes tears of awe and joy,—is that I have not done anything to deserve being loved in that unconditional way. I have discovered God's personal love for me. Of course, there is something I can do to open myself up to this divine, unconditional love, namely, by sharing myself. Others will love me when I do that, for real love is interpersonal communion. That is what Jesus was telling Martha. Mary chose "the better part" by communing with Jesus. Through that dialogue she could discover the mystery of divine love in Jesus, and also in her own heart.

Grace is a discovery that I am loved not because of what I have done for God or for others, but because of WHO I am. My personal identity,—indeed my first name,—is why I am loved. This is to know LOVE, the true love that is pure gift. Anything less than pure gift is not really love. It may be appreciation, or intimacy, or a helping attitude, but only as pure gift does it deserve the name love. I decide to love the other by making a gift of my love. This is something that all of us need to learn. It is basic to understanding Jesus' gospel.

We see this divine love in the way Jesus related to his disciples. He did not usually work miracles for them the way he did for others. He communicated his love to them by *sharing himself* with them. He said they would know he was their friend by the fact that he shared with them all that the Father had revealed to him in his heart (Jn 15:15), which included Jesus' thoughts, feelings, hopes, temptations, and especially his INNER LIGHT. He also loved them by affirming them. He really believed in each of his disciples, saying that they would do all that he did, and even greater things (Jn 14:12). Far from making them dependent on what he could do for them, he wanted them to believe they would receive his same

Holy Spirit, and then be able to go out on mission on their own (Mt 10:1).

What TWOS need is to see themselves as very special and unique persons because of what *they* feel and what *they* experience. They also need to grow in the humility of knowing they have needs which are to be cared for by others. If as a TWO I don't let others care for me, how can they get close to me? If I don't share myself by telling others my needs and hurts, how will I ever experience being loved just because of WHO I am?

## PASSAGES FOR MEDITATION

Wedding Reception at Cana—John 2:1-11.
Cure of Peter's Mother-in-law—Mark 1:29-34.
Jesus Visits Mary and Martha—Luke 10:38-42.

## QUESTIONS FOR DIALOGUE

1. How do we love people in ways other than through serving their needs?
2. Where do we see people making the mistake of trying to *win* love from others, such as their children, by what they do for them?
3. What does it mean to *choose* to love someone?

### THREE: His Ambition

THREES have a great deal of *ambition* to succeed in whatever they undertake to do. They plan carefully and expect their co-workers to be competent and dedicated. For THREES, to be is to be successful, and this success depends on the favorable reaction of others.

Jesus himself had great ambition to succeed in what he set out to do. His concern to succeed as a young man brought about what he called his temptations from Satan. Like all THREES, he needed to struggle against the temptation for success in the eyes of the world. We see this indicated by his experience in the desert:

> Then Jesus was led up into the desert by the Spirit to be tempted by the devil. After having fasted forty days and forty nights, he was hungry.
> The tempter approached him and said: "If you are the Son of God, command these stones to become bread."
> Jesus answered: "It has been written: 'We do not live only on bread, but on every word coming from the mouth of God.'"
> Then the devil took him into the holy city, and stood him on the wing of the temple and said to him: "If you are the Son of God, jump down; for it has been written: 'He will give orders to his angels concerning you, and they will hold you in their hands, lest your feet trip against a stone.'"
> Jesus said to him: "It has also been written: 'Don't overtempt the Lord your God.'"
> Then the devil took him to an exceedingly high mountain, and showed him all the kingdoms of the world and their glory. And he said to Jesus: "All this I will give you if you fall down and worship me."
> Then Jesus said to him: "Go away, Satan, for it has been written: 'You shall worship the Lord your God and serve only him.'"
> The devil then left him, and angels approached and ministered to him. (Mt 4:1-11)

Jesus had been impressed by the success of the prophet John. People from all over the land had been going down to the Jordan to listen to John's preaching. Many were reforming their ways. Even Herod's soldiers were asking John how to prepare for the coming of the Kingdom of God.

Jesus had placed himself at John's feet, offering his whole life to God for the coming of the Kingdom. After having been baptized by John, he came up out of the river, and while at prayer his whole being was opened to the Father (Lk 3:21f). He experienced being endowed with all the gifts and powers he would need for his mission. He felt confident he could develop and use these gifts for the coming of the Kingdom on earth, especially because he knew the Father believed in him.

After returning from the desert, he immediately began preaching the message of the Kingdom. He used the same words John had used so effectively: "Repent, the Kingdom of God is at hand!" (Mk 1:14) Unlike John, however, he was not going to remain in the desert and wait for people to come to him. Instead he went out to the people, wherever they were.

There had been a big change in Jesus at the time of his baptism. He had suddenly become a very public person. When he went back to Nazareth, the opinion of the people there was that he was pretending to be someone he was not. They were not ready to accept him as a prophet sent from God, and so they refused to take to heart his message. Jesus passed it off by saying: "A prophet is not accepted by his own townspeople" (Lk 4:22).

After John had been martyred, Jesus drew to himself many of John's disciples. They had received good religious training from John, and had grown in faith through a discipline similar to life in a monastery like that of nearby Qumran. Jesus, however, was not going to let them continue being like monks; they were going to be missionaries, travelling salespersons for the Kingdom.

## His Leadership Qualities

To succeed in his mission, Jesus developed his personality to be a leader. He became an *attention-getter*. Far from being a religious recluse, he was very active, always on the move. He was direct with people; he looked them in the eyes, and responded according to the way they approached him.

He made himself *available*. He had no office hours and indeed no office. He even gave up having a home of his own, — as he said: "the Son of Man has no place to lay his head" (Mt 8:20). The foxes, he said, had more than he, because they had their dens. His remaining unmarried was an asset to this availability. People of every economic and social status felt they could approach him and that he would have time for them.

He *loved people*. He sought the comradeship not only of men but also of women. He had women disciples (cf Lk 8:1-3), such as Mary and Martha of Bethany, and enjoyed spending time with them. Both women and men found him *exciting* to be with. They also appreciated his *fearlessness* in facing people, a quality which made them feel secure when they dedicated themselves to follow him.

Jesus was a great *communicator*. He was able to

attract thousands of people to listen to his teaching. By using parables he challenged people to make their own decision, rather than to accept a decision made for them. They accepted his leadership because he brought hope and spoke of *good news*. He worked at being a good salesman. To achieve success, he put a great deal of effort into making an impression on others. He was completely convinced of the message he preached. He attracted people to that message by the best advertising the world has ever seen: MIRACLES! Would they otherwise have listened? He kept connecting these wonders with the message he brought.

Jesus was always IN CHARGE. He called his followers "sheep" and he their "shepherd". The apostles later gave a gentle connotation to these terms, as part of the message of Jesus as savior, who protects the sheep against the wolves and goes to rescue the straying. However, the terms themselves also made clear who was *boss*. He was their leader, and they followed his teaching and his example. What attracted them were the values he stood for and lived out. For these values they also would make great sacrifices, even that of giving up their lives. Jesus knew that a leader needs to communicate clearly to others the values he lives for, and to be able somehow to touch people to bind themselves together for the sake of upholding, living out, and promoting these values. The values he radiated had their source in himself. They were all summed up in what Jesus called "The Kingdom of God."

That Kingdom was already present in Jesus himself, as evidenced by Jesus' ability to bring about healing in people, both in their bodies and souls. The Kingdom was also present in his expectations: it was to come on earth. Later he would put his own Spirit powerfully within his followers so that they would continue to manifest and to promote the presence of God's promised reign. Being the source of the message of the new life, Jesus accepted the position of being the leader of what he called "his little flock". This became the very meaning and purpose of his life.

As a good leader, Jesus knew how to train co-workers. First of all, he himself *chose* his collaborators. He did not leave it up to them to choose him. As he said, "You did not choose me: I chose you to go out and bear much fruit" (Jn 15:16). To these chosen collaborators he explained everything about his vision and values. Although he did not expect the crowds who listened to his preaching to understand everything he said, he did expect that of his co-workers. As soon as he chose them, he also gave them responsibility to do some of the work he had been doing. He insisted he was giving them all the skills they needed to do this work. He gave them oil to heal the sick and insisted they would even be able to do miracles as he did. They were to have confidence they could do works of God in his name, even to the extent of overcoming demonic forces. When they returned very enthusiastic about how successful they had been, he rejoiced with them, and prayed out loud in thanksgiving to the Father for having given such gifts to his comrades (Lk 10:21).

From his co-workers he chose a central staff of twelve. These would have a special position and ministry. They would be the foundation for the worldwide expansion of his movement. He knew that a strong central organization was necessary to preserve the original message and ensure the unity of all the eventual followers among all the peoples of the world. That the central staff was twelve was symbolic, and indicated the reunion of the twelve tribes of Israel, once dispersed abroad, but now through the promised Messiah reunited as a single people to serve as a light to all nations.

All these activities and attitudes of Jesus were included in his campaign to influence the whole world. Although it all was in God's hands, as a human protagonist in history he knew he needed to set in motion historical forces which could change the way people would live in the future. He needed co-workers, and he needed them to be organized and empowered to influence others with the message to which they had committed their lives.

## The Trap of Living for Success

THREES are often criticized for making their work their life. Although this is true, is it really all that bad? Jesus, we see, lived for the success of his movement. His life was his work. He sacrificed everything for the success of his mission, and also *expected this of his followers.*

Another alleged fault of THREES is their intolerance with incompetence. If a worker is sick for some length of time, they will simply want him or her replaced. It puzzles them when an employee seems to need a lot of personal time. THREES see life as lived for the success of their undertakings. They have little patience in valuing anything above competence, even that of seniority. They put their feelings into a sack when it comes to administration, though they will be fair and objective toward each co-worker.

The main trap of THREES, however, is their avoidance of failure, which they see as a very great evil. To them their own WORTH is at stake when there is the prospect of failing.

What is success? In the final analysis *success depends on what others think!* Should you be told by such a person that it is important that you give a "very good talk" at a certain meeting, what is being said is that your talk is to *please* your hearers. What is successful, and thus "good", is what pleases others.

Another problem in making one's goal in life the achieving of success and avoiding failure is that the quest is never satisfied. Somehow there is never enough success. There needs to be one success after another. This too indicates that such motivation is a trap, not only because it depends on what pleases others but also because one's heart somehow is never satisfied with whatever success is attained.

## How Jesus Dealt with Failure

This trap of the THREE is the avoidance of failure. Jesus himself did not view failure as the supreme evil. His dealing with his own failure in his endeavors serves as a model for us. This is especially so from the fact that he told his followers that they should be ready to experience in their lives failure like his own. This would happen precisely because they had committed themselves to following him. It was the cost of being a disciple (Lk 14:25–33).

There is reason to believe that initially in his public life Jesus expected he would be successful in bringing about the Kingdom of God. He did achieve an enormous popular response early in his ministry. He quickly got disciples, he displayed great power in working miracles, and thousands followed him to hear the word of God from his lips.

This all went sour one fateful day in Galilee. Jesus had decided that he and his disciples needed a rest, at least for a day. They got into a boat at Capernaum and headed across the Lake of Genesareth to a desert area (Mk 6:31ff). As they went along, however, crowds of people from the villages around began following them along the shore, so that when they came ashore with the boat all these people were waiting for them. Jesus immediately gave up the idea of a free day. All that day he taught them. One can imagine what energy and skill it took to speak for hours before all these thousands and to keep their attention. As evening came on Jesus became concerned with the fact they had not eaten since they had left their homes that morning. He then fed them in a miraculous multiplication of bread and fish a boy had brought along, perhaps as a peddler, or simply for lunch. Initially the crowd did not know a miracle was happening, but after all had eaten. they saw that the baskets of leftovers were much greater than the lunch basket of bread and fish provided by the boy. They began to talk excitedly about what had happened and what it meant. Someone began to caucus. They sensed that here was their opportunity to overthrow the Roman domination of their country: they would start a movement to set up Jesus as their king sent from God! (Jn 6:14f)

Jesus became frightened when he saw what was happening among the crowd. He insisted that his disciples get into the boat,—without any questions asked,—and had them leave the area. He did not want to lose his faithful followers by letting them get sucked into these plans for a revolution. Then he managed to persuade the crowd to disperse and go back home.

Once alone he climbed up the mountainside and spent a long time in prayer under the night sky. He had a lot to pray about, for all his own plans were crumbling. In actual fact he had *failed* to become the leader of these people. They had not subscribed to his vision or his values. Misunderstanding his mission, they wanted to *use* his closeness to God for their own political purposes. As he had told his disciples, it was a temptation from the devil for him to aspire to become a political leader, for that was not the correct interpretation of what the promised Messiah was to be.

Through his prayer that night Jesus decided he would have to leave Galilee and go up to Jerusalem to make a fresh start. He had failed, yes, but now he would start again, this time not with the multitudes of people from small towns like his own Nazareth, but with those who were well schooled in Judaism and the scriptures. He would go to the leaders at Jerusalem and make his teaching clear to them, thereby giving them every opportunity to know him as he was and to understand all he taught. In this way they would have a choice either to accept him or to reject him.

Jesus sensed that he would also fail in Jerusalem. From such failure, however, the good he sought would come. It was shown in the scriptures that this would be God's way of bringing liberation to his people. The Son of Man, as Jesus said, must be first rejected and killed, but then he would be raised up to his glory (Lk 18:31-33).

It was Jesus' mission to reveal in the paschal mystery that success comes out of failure. Often God shows his greatest power in our lives only when we have suffered some great disappointment, even to the extent of failing in all we have worked to achieve. Far from such failure being a sign of God abandoning us, he is putting into effect his plan to bring success out of failure. For those who choose success as the goal of their lives, to follow the footsteps of Jesus in bearing their own cross may well be the acceptance of failure in the enterprise into which they have put their life's blood.

Such acceptance of failure is to include faith that the failure is not a sign God is turning away from them. God did not turn away from Jesus hanging on the cross, even though Jesus shouted to his divine Father: "Why have you abandoned me?" (Mk 15:34) As the author of the Letter to the Hebrews says, God did hear Jesus' prayer for help, and later raised him from the dead (Heb 5:7). It could very well be that through our abandonment to God we find that at times we must accept great losses in our lives. Later on, however, we may find that God has restored to us, like he did to Job, what we lost. More often, however, it is through failures that we discover a new power of serving others and a new motivation for living which is no longer for what we once considered "success", but now centers on the gift of ourselves for the building of God's own kingdom.

## PASSAGES FOR MEDITATION

The Baptism of Jesus—Matthew 3:1-17.
Jesus Rejected at Nazareth—Luke 4:14-30.
The Return of the Seventy-two—Luke 10:17-24.
Jesus Feeds the Five Thousand—John 6:1-15.
The Cost of Being a Disciple—Luke 14:25-33.

## QUESTIONS FOR DIALOGUE

1. How important is it to have clear goals in our lives? What are some goals of others that we especially admire?
2. What are some common temptations to make the end justify the means?
3. How have we experienced *failure* as a way of carrying our own cross while following the footsteps of Jesus?

## FOUR: His Sensitivity

Jesus could well be called "the patron of misunderstood people." He frequently complained to his closest friends that they did not understand him. A reason for this was his acute sensitivity. One example of such sensitive feelings was demonstrated during the banquet held for him at Bethany shortly before he was arrested and crucified:

> As Jesus was reclining at table at the house of Simon the Leper in Bethany, a woman came to him with an alabaster jar of very expensive ointment which she poured over his head. When they saw this the disciples became angry and said: "Why is this being wasted? This could be sold for a lot of money and that could be given to the poor." Knowing this, Jesus said to them: "Why do you trouble the woman? She did a good deed to me. You will always have the poor among you, but you will not always have me. This woman has put this ointment on my body to prepare me for burial. Truly I tell you, what she has done will be spoken of in memory of her wherever in the whole world this gospel is proclaimed (Mt 26:6–13).

This story unfolds at a very critical time in his life. He and his disciples had been going to Jerusalem each morning and then returning to Bethany at night to relax and rest at the home of Martha. The conspiracy against Jesus was growing, and these days were nerve-racking for him. Pharisees and sadducees were trying to trip him up to get a case against him for his arrest. Jesus knew very well that they were going to succeed in their scheme. Each evening, emotionally exhausted, he walked back the three miles to Bethany. On one such evening a banquet was held at Bethany for him and his apostles. During the banquet a woman friend of his came into the room, opened up an

alabaster jar of precious ointment she was carrying
and poured the fragrant oil over his head as a gesture
of deep affection and care. She knew that Jesus
needed something more than a party to lift his spirits.
She wanted him to know that she understood the
pressure and sadness in his life. He needed to feel
cared for.

While she was doing this the apostles began to
whisper about this great "waste" of precious ointment that could have been sold in order to give the
money to the poor. Jesus at once stood and told his
apostles to stop troubling the woman. He said that
what she had done was "beautiful." It represented, he
said, a preparation of his body for burial. There
would be other times when they could help the poor.
The poor would always be with them, but he was
about to leave them.

Jesus felt very misunderstood. Could not they sense
how heavy his heart was? They were begrudging him
this gesture of love from his woman friend! He would
not always be with them! After he was gone they
could give away money to the poor! This body of his
they see would soon be in the grave. It would be so
soon that they could think of this anointing as a
preparation of his body for burial. Couldn't they
understand how hard it was for him to know he was
to die and leave them?

He also wanted to defend her and the great value
of her expression of love to him. He said that what
she had done was "beautiful", a word not recorded of
Jesus elsewhere in the scriptures. To emphasize how
he felt he declared that her expression of love would
be remembered wherever his gospel was preached

until the end of time. To him their reaction showed great insensitivity both to his own feelings and to those of the woman.

## The Last Supper

A few days later Jesus held his Last Supper for these same apostles, and in the course of the meal he got up, donned a towel, and went around the table washing their feet and drying them with the towel (Jn 13:4ff). Here again he felt misunderstood. He had arranged the whole supper that they would remember these last hours with him and the great love he had for them, but they did not understand how hard it was for him to take leave of them.

As is characteristic of FOURS, Jesus found leave-taking very difficult and something that needed a lot of time to be expressed. How could he ever express adequately what they meant to him and how it hurt him to go away? The apostles had followed all his instructions to arrange the supper but had not followed the feelings of his heart. He did not mean his leave-taking to be sad; in fact, it needed to be celebrated, and in a way that they would always remember. It was his wish that all his future followers would remember this night by repeating it as a ritual meal (Lk 22:19).

In the course of the supper Jesus talked mainly of love: of the love he had for the Father, and of his love for them, his friends, shown by his dying for them (Jn 15:12–17). They were to be faithful to him by show-ing to one another the love he had shown to them. It was disappointing to him, though, that in the actual celebration of the supper so much of what he held in his heart escaped them, even though he conveyed these feelings with dramatic and unusual gestures. They seemed so unfeeling and insensitive to these signs of parting! Were they simply not letting the meaning come through because they could not give up their own image of who and what he was to be? At any rate, it all added to his loneliness and feeling of being abandoned. They were not with him in their hearts at this most tragic moment of his life experience.

After the supper, he took his apostles to the garden of Gethsemane (Mt 26:36–46; Mk 14:32–42; Lk 22:39–46). He selected Peter, James, and John to go apart with him. He sensed a need to pray to his Father in solitude, and yet needed the company of his closest followers. As anguish came over him, he told them that he felt that he was *dying* of sadness. He went a few steps away and fell on his knees, pleading in prayer to the Father to deliver him from this hour. The anguish was so overwhelming that his own blood mingled with his cold perspiration. When he got up and returned he found his three friends asleep! How could their hearts be so insensitive? Why could they not be with him in this tragic hour? Was he to be that abandoned and forsaken? He asked them why they could not watch one hour with him, and told them they needed to stay awake at this crucial moment, and pray that they not fall into temptation.

## Other Times of Tears

This had not been the first time Jesus was in tears. As a very sensitive person, Jesus often expressed his sadness and grief by weeping. There was the morning some days before, when Jesus had been on his way to Jerusalem from Bethany. As he had passed along the side of the Mount of Olives overlooking the city, and looked at the temple below, he suddenly stopped and burst into tears. He was thinking of the future when the city would be besieged and destroyed by a foreign army. He saw this as a consequence of the people rejecting him. Through his tears he said that he had wanted to protect them and hold them close to himself as a mother hen gathers her chicks under her wings, but they would not let him (Lk 19:41–44).

Another occasion of his weeping was at the tomb of Lazarus. As told to us in John 11:1–44, Mary and Martha sent Jesus a message saying cryptically: "He whom you love is sick." Knowing Jesus' fondness for Mary and Martha, the disciples were surprised he did not set out at once for Bethany to be at the bedside of Lazarus. Jesus, however, delayed for several days before setting out. As he approached Bethany, only Martha came out to greet him. Her sister Mary remained grieving in the house. Jesus was in trouble in his relationship with Mary and Martha, for during his delay in Judea their brother Lazarus had died and was already buried. The first words Martha said to Jesus when she met him was: "Lord, if you had been here our brother would never have died." Jesus replied with some words about her brother rising again, but to Martha this was little consolation, since Jesus could have prevented his death. She said she knew we are all going to rise again at the end of the world. Jesus then asked where Mary was, so Martha went to get her. As soon as Martha whispered to Mary that the Lord was asking for her, Mary got up and went out to Jesus. Her first words were the same as Martha's: "Lord, if you had been here our brother would never have died." The women who had followed her out of the house all began to weep. Their grief touched Jesus deeply, and with a sigh he began to weep with them. Going to the place of burial, he had the stone rolled away from the tomb and then called into the tomb for Lazarus to come out. There was a rustle, and then the figure of Lazarus came forth through the opening, completely bound up with burial cloths. Jesus gave the order that he be freed of his bindings.

## His Sense of Drama

Not only did the raising of Lazarus reveal a sensitivity in Jesus demonstrated by tears, but it also was a great dramatic performance. Never before in the history of the world had anything been performed like this in a cemetery. The body of Lazarus had been long enough in the tomb to be full of maggots. Martha, with her customary directness, had told Jesus that there would be a very bad smell if they rolled back the stone. Before shouting into the tomb Jesus expressed certitude that his command would bring forth Lazarus. Even in his prayer to the Father preceding his command that Lazarus come forth, Jesus said that he knew the Father would hear this prayer of his, because the Father always heard his prayers. He was praying out loud so those around would know his closeness to the Father. The gospel writer continually reminds us in the course of this story that Jesus *intended* to make the raising of Lazarus *very dramatic*. It was characteristic of Jesus that he would want to do so.

In the course of the same week preceding his arrest, Jesus had arranged a procession proclaiming himself as the Messiah coming into the city of Jerusalem (Mt 21:1-11; Mk 11:1-11; Lk 19:28-40; Jn 12:12-19). As the scriptures had foretold, the promised savior would come humbly into the city, riding on an ass. Jesus arranged this whole scenario, but it was not simply a *performance*. He was living out his real life as he was fulfilling the scriptures in a dramatic way. He expressed outwardly by riding an ass the way he felt inwardly about being the Messiah. Kings and princes rode into their city mounted on stately horses, adding to their majesty above the people. Jesus rode an ass, not as a comic figure, but as the savior of those who believed in him. He saved them by being close to them, by being on their level. *Majesty* could be appropriate for God as creator and judge over all, but it was not the way for being "God who saves", the very meaning of Jesus' name.

In the course of his public ministry Jesus had had a practice of using dramatic gestures in connection with his actions of healing. He did not simply use words to give commands for healing, but liked to heal by touching people. In healing the man born deaf and dumb, Jesus put his finger into the man's ears, touched the man's tongue, and then said loudly, "Ephatha," meaning "Be opened!" (Mk 7:34). He healed a man born blind from birth by picking up some dirt, spitting into it to make mud, dabbing that on the man's eyes, and then telling him to go and wash in the pool of Siloam (Jn 9:6). Such dramatic gestures aroused faith in the person, but also were natural to the way Jesus expressed himself and his inner power.

The gospels depict Jesus' human body as having a power of healing, as is shown in the story of the woman suffering from a flow of blood (Mk 5:25–34). She believed that if she touched only the hem of his garment she would be healed. As she touched his garment while a crowd was pressing about him, Jesus felt power go out from him. Christians should see Jesus as giving an example in how to minister to the sick and handicapped. Healing through the power of Jesus is to be conveyed in tactile and even dramatic ways, especially within the ecclesial rituals we call sacraments, which are done expressly in the name of Jesus.

## The Shadow of FOURS

The influence of our shadow is shown by the way we seek to manipulate or "overshadow" others. One way this is seen in FOURS is by *snobbishness*. This arises from the importance FOURS give to refinement and good taste. They tend to look down on people who give little attention to what is elegant and beautiful. Along with such snobbishness, FOURS sometimes surprise us with their tendency to be envious of others who get more attention, whether from their style of dress, their personality, or anything else that stands out about them. Envy seems so unworthy of FOURS because it is so base to begrudge others for being outstanding. Real refinement of our person ought to be characterized by rejoicing in the goodness and attention granted to others because we love them.

The greatest trap of FOURS, however is using melancholy and self-pity as a way to draw attention to themselves. It is a way of feeling very "special" as a person. By sighs and tears they share their feelings about past tragedies in life, and thereby dominate another by engendering sympathy. One of the favorite themes in romantic literature has been that of the misunderstood person of fragile health who withdrew from normal life and then sucked into his or her life some generous soul. The one who tried to understand and be a friend was drawn into a pit of sadness and isolation, leading to a tragic and senseless death.

### Jesus' Avoidance of Self-pity

As we study Jesus, we see that even as "a man of sorrows" he consistently avoided the trap of self-pity. Whenever Jesus spoke to his disciples of his coming suffering and death, he added also the prediction that he would rise again (Mk 8:31;10:32-34). He thus looked forward to it not as ultimate tragedy, but rather as a victory. He called it another "baptism" (Lk 12:50). It was an hour of darkness, but only an "hour", that is, a brief time, and then he would have victory over the powers of darkness and death. He liked to compare this tragic hour to a mother's labor pains. At the time when the labor began she was sad, but once her baby was born she forgot what the pain had been because she was so happy to have brought new life into the world (Jn 16:21).

Jesus also avoided portraying himself as a lone, tragic figure. He said that if others had persecuted him, they would persecute his followers even more. He even said that to follow him his disciples would have to carry a *daily* cross behind him (Lk 14:27ff). Before pledging to be his followers they were to sit down and consider if they were willing to pay the price of discipleship. The forces opposed to him in his *hour* would sooner or later conspire against them. Like a general opposing an enemy army, they were to consider if they had enough resources for the battle. If not, they had best send out messengers to accommodate themselves with the enemy rather than face him. It was worth one's life to try to build up God's Kingdom, but anyone doing that needed to be ready to suffer for it as Jesus himself had suffered.

As Jesus had become more and more aware of the growing conspiracy against him he had not run into hiding with his friends for protection. He went to Jerusalem, which was the home turf of his enemies. He faced them daily, argued with them, and tried to change their attitudes towards his gospel. He wanted to make clear to them who he was and what he stood for. Instead of brooding about others being against him and failing to recognize his innocence and goodness, he sought to meet people as long as he still enjoyed the light of day (Jn 12:35f). Despite the pressures against him, Jesus intended to do as much good as he could as long as he could. As his enemies gathered their forces against him, he did not fall into melancholy or despair. Instead, he reacted by increasing his activity in Jerusalem. If he could not touch their *hearts* by healing miracles, he would try at least to touch their *minds* by logic. Rather than cling to his friends for support, he tried to prepare them for the approaching trauma of his death. They would all be scattered, he said, because he, their shepherd, would be struck down (Mk 14:27). For this reason he insisted that they care for one another by sharing with one another the same love he had given to them. (Jn 15:12). At the moment of his arrest, he spoke up for them to his captors, asking that as his disciples they be allowed to escape (Jn 18:8).

## PASSAGES FOR MEDITATION

The Woman Who Touched Jesus' Cloak—Mark 5: 25-34.
At the Tomb of Lazarus—John 11:1-44.
The Triumphant Entry into Jerusalem—Matthew 21:1-11.
Jesus Washes His Disciples' Feet—John 13:1-17.
The New Commandment—John 15:9-17.
Jesus Prays at Gethsemane—Mark 14:32-42.

## QUESTIONS FOR DIALOGUE

1. What are some good characteristics about persons we know who are very sensitive? How would we like to imitate them?
2. What advice would we give to people who are hypersensitive and easily hurt?
3. How would we like to see more feeling expressed in our religion?

## FIVE: His Wisdom

To see Jesus as a FIVE, we need to notice his great concern for wisdom. Like all FIVES, it was very important to Jesus to be wise, and not foolish. He also insisted on it for his disciples, as is shown in this concluding passage from the Sermon on the Mount:

> Everyone, therefore, who hears these words of mine and acts on them will be likened to a wise man who built his home on rock. Then the rain came down and the rivers came and the winds blew, all lashing against that home, but it did not fall, for it had been founded on rock. But everyone who hears these words of mine and does not act on them will be likened to a foolish men who built his home on sand. Then the rain came down and the rivers came and the winds blew, all beating against that home, and it fell with a great crash. (Matthew 7:24-29)

Here Jesus is telling us to put priorities in our life. The foolish person experiences life as "just one damn thing after another." Wise people try to build their lives on chosen goals and values. They don't let life just happen, nor do they necessarily follow patterns of behavior taken for granted by others around them. To build one's life on rock involves living for values greater than oneself or any passing pleasure.

To know what values to choose as priorities, we need to know and reflect on what we know. Our modern society may have a hankering for reflection, but the pace of life and the priority of getting something done often eats away at one's ability to stop in order to look and listen inside oneself. Gaining wisdom is always a matter of listening to various voices, both from without and within, and being able to sift out what is best. Wisdom is a knowledge that leads to correct judgment, especially as to what values we should incarnate in our lives. After all, it is wise to live for a purpose, especially a purpose which involves a universal vision.

Lack of reflection leads to foolishness, to reacting without thinking of purposes and goals. Jesus considered foolishness to be a vice, even though probably few confession lists of sins include it. He placed foolishness alongside greed, indecency, blasphemy, arrogance, and other "evil things" that might lodge in our hearts and defile us (Mk 7:22f).

Jesus' own quest for wisdom involved thinking things out for himself. He often sought out lonely places for such reflection on the scriptures, on his life, and on the will of God. As is characteristic of a wise man he knew more than he said, or at least waited for the right moment to share his truth.

Because he thought out things for himself, the crowds found a freshness and newness in his teaching, in contrast to the rabbis, whose teaching method was to cite various authorities on a given case. Jesus put himself on the line by speaking out of his own reflection. For this reason he gained the reputation of teaching "with authority" (Mt:7:29).

That "authority" was the conviction he expressed. It came from what he called an interior "living water" (Jn 7:38). It was a power within himself to reflect on what he had read and seen in such a way that he came to see what was right and best. This inner power was also described as "light" because it gave clarity to his thinking and teaching. Far from simply being a matter of ideals and theories, his teaching was always practical. Wisdom has that effect.

## Reflective Principles

As is characteristic in anyone trying to share wisdom with others, Jesus liked to express what was right and best through pithy statements or proverbs. These were meant to be reflective principles to aid others in gaining wisdom through reflecting on their lives. These principles are quite different from commandments or laws, and the very formulation Jesus gave them could cause a person to ponder and seek to understand more.

Among such gospel proverbs or maxims are the following:

> Many who now are first will be last and the last first (Mk 10:31).
> Judge not that you be not judged (Mt 7:1).
> My yoke is easy and my burden light (Mt 11:32).

Jesus considered statements like these a means for evangelization. As reflective principles, they are best explicated through anecdotes or parables, which, in turn, lead to reflection on our experience. Their purpose is to lead us to the wisdom of doing our own thinking.

That the last will be first and the first last is like the story of two nuns who worked their whole life in the convent kitchen. It was often hard and thankless work but they encouraged one another to remember that they would be rewarded in heaven. They found it especially hard not to complain when the bishop came for a banquet and received so much attention and honor, while nobody even noticed them and the work they did to prepare the meal.

The day did arrive when they both reached heaven and all their unnoticed labors were indeed richly rewarded by the Lord. Their contentment was upset, however, when angels came around one day with banners and flags, and announced that a big parade was to happen that day. The angels explained that the celebration was for a bishop who had just arrived in heaven. Quite annoyed, the nuns told the angels that they did not think it was fair that after they had given bishops so much attention and honor on earth that they should now be called upon to do the same thing in heaven. To this the angels replied that they needed a celebration, "because," as they said, "it is so rare that a bishop arrives here."

Both this story and the statement about the first and last would have us reflect that honor in this world may not lead to honor in the next, and that many who are unnoticed here on earth will be in high honor in heaven. C.S. Lewis in his Narnia adventures liked to portray the same truth about who would be exulted and who brought low in the next world. One of his stories has a taxi driver and his wife, both with cockney accents, being chosen as king and queen of Narnia.

The second statement,—about judging and being judged,—is like the story of a Catholic mother who lost her teenage son in a car accident. Her pastor refused to have a funeral mass for the boy because he said she had not paid her pew rent. A fundamentalist minister agreed to have the funeral. Subsequently she joined his church and now tries to get her brothers and sisters to leave the Catholic Church because, she says, it will lead them to hell.

This true story, which took place many years after Vatican II, points out the evil of churchmen making judgments on who is in the state of grace, when such judgment really can be made only by God.

As regards the third statement, to take on Jesus' yoke could mean that he is pulling our burden with us so that we form a team pulling the load. It may be better explicated, however, by a dream a woman had of walking across the sand. Looking back, she saw two sets of footprints, and understood this to mean that Jesus walked with her in her life. As she walked along, suddenly the going became very, very difficult, and she struggled and suffered to continue. Looking back then, she saw only one set of footprints. She complained to the Lord: "Why did you leave me when life became so hard?" Jesus replied that the single set of footprints were really his, for he was carrying her.

## The Trap of Aloofness

Because the attainment of wisdom requires a great deal of time for salutary reflection, there is the danger of becoming too aloof. FIVES, in their quest to understand more, tend to be always looking for time alone. They become quickly bored with cocktail parties and small talk, and see nothing wrong in simply "checking-out" without saying anything to anyone, so tht they can get back to their current project of study. When they don't find being with others of use in learning anything, they see no reason to waste their time by remaining. Similarly, they may join a group already in session and just quietly observe.

FIVES have a problem in tending to be *observers* of life rather than *participants*. They leave it up to others to initiate and carry out social activities, for they themselves are busy at their study and reflection. Their inner world so fascinates them then it often preoccupies their attention. This also gives them a poor sense of the present. They fail to remember names. They tend to speak in monotone.

Because depth of reflection is so important to them, they take pride in looking at anything from all possible points of view. Most other people, in their opinion, are very *shallow* in their thinking. They see evidence of this when they try to explain what they have been thinking about: instead of being interested, others just look bored, or drift away. For FIVES to share what they are *thinking* means laying out what amounts to a treatise, which isn't what most people are accustomed to converse about, especially at a party. An added problem is that FIVES are *loners* in the way they go about study. Consequently, the only way another can talk with them intellectually is to use their categories. They push personal reflection to an excess in a world that requires a cooperative and collaborative spirit.

*Jesus Not a Loner*

Although he was very dedicated to solitary contemplation and to thinking things out by himself, Jesus was never what one would call a "loner." As a man dedicated to wisdom he knew he needed disciples. So important was this that he actually left his own home in Nazareth, and his occupation as carpenter, in order not only to be a wandering prophet but especially to live with his followers day and night. In all of this camping out and walking the roadways of Galilee and Judea, he spent most of his time with them, and not with the crowds who were especially attracted to him as a miracle-worker.

He constantly entered into dialogue with these disciples, typically asking them questions and drawing out their responses. This then gave him an opening for further reflection with them. A great deal of Jesus' teaching handed down to us in the gospels came from table conversation, rather than from formal discourses. His teachings were in bits and pieces, leaving the gospel redactors the theological task of stringing them together in an interpretative pattern, something like the beads of a necklace. This piecemeal way of instruction stemming from dialogue was the way a guru would teach, for the events of life and occasional conversations were the place where God's hand was to be seen. Jesus wanted his followers to discover wisdom from the school of life, where the Kingdom of God was already coming into fulfillment according to God's pre-arranged Plan. To ascertain the mysteries of the Kingdom the disciples needed to experience events surrounding Jesus and then to reflect on them to see the action of God. The world was diaphanous, but it took spiritual insight to see through events and thereby join God in his action in the world. Jesus called this the coming of the Kingdom of heaven.

Sometimes an ordinary event was used by Jesus for a moral teaching, such as when some men took for granted they would eat at the head table (Lk 14:7ff), or when a widow living in poverty put two copper coins into the collection box at the Temple (Lk 21:1ff). As a guru Jesus could find events around him filled with moral lessons. His style was to take advantage of what happened in daily life to school his disciples in greater understanding of God's ways.

This practise of Jesus points to the great importance of being a participant in life rather than simply an observer. Since God is the Lord of history and is at work in the world fulfilling his Plan to bring about his Kingdom as a transformation of human society, it would be very foolish to try to attain wisdom simply by the study of what is printed in books. The most important realities of life are to be known only by participating in them. One can gain information and analyze problems by merely being an attentive observer, but what are called "mysteries" can be known only by personal involvement.

An obvious example of this is that love cannot be known by studying about it, or even by defining it. If we don't know what love is without a definition we will never learn what it is from a definition. To be able to articulate the experience of love is important, but before you can do that with much benefit you first need to know what love is by personal experience. The wise person, schooled by life, knows that. Not to know it is to miss the wisdom one may be trying so very hard to attain through reading and thinking.

Jesus enjoyed praying alone for long hours, and his disciples were fascinated by the depth of concentration they observed in him when he was at prayer. Such prayer was imperative for Jesus in order for him to complete the mission assigned to him as the Messiah promised in the scriptures. It meant he needed to reflect on events as they unfolded in his life in the light of the grace given him by the indwelling Spirit. Yet we never see Jesus perturbed when he is interrupted by his disciples while in the midst of prayer. He loved them very much and was grateful they were with him. He was also aware that the event of their interrupting him could be an intervention of the Kingdom of God. He did say they were all given to him by the Father (Jn 17:6). They were also given to him that day as they interrupted his prayer. For Jesus, "interruptions were his schedule."

## PASSAGES FOR MEDITATION

The Things That Make a Person Unclean—Mark 7:1-23.
Judge Not That You Be Not Judged—Matthew 7:1-5.
Come to Me and Rest—Matthew 11:25-30.
Humility and Hospitality—Luke 14:7-14.
The Widow's Offering—Luke 21:1-4.

## QUESTIONS FOR DIALOGUE

1. Which teachings of Jesus have I tried to build my life on? How have they helped me during the "storms" of my life?

2. How do we experience prayer as a time for reflection on our lives in the light of Jesus' teachings?
3. What are some ways of entering into dialogue with others in order to lead them to greater wisdom?

## SIX: His Loyalty

Each of the Enneagram types defines being a person differently. "To be" may be "to be perfect" (ONES), "to be helpful" (TWOS), "to be successful" (THREES), "to be special" (FOURS), "to be wise" (FIVES), "to be responsible" (SIXES), "to be cheerful" (SEVENS), "to be strong" (EIGHTS), or "to be content" (NINES). It is out of how we think of ourselves as a person that is derived our general behavior and attitudes that make up what we call our personality. Our behavior is, in fact, a sign of what we think of ourselves. This is particularly true as regards SIXES. For them, to be responsible and loyal defines who they are and what they do.

SIXES see life as filled with demands. They go about their days seeking to respond to such demands. They see life as holding them accountable for doing what they are supposed to do.

Jesus had such a sense of responsibility. His greatest expression of being accountable was letting himself be crucified. While hanging from the cross he continued to fulfill what was demanded of him as he understood it. An example of this are the words he spoke from the cross to his mother and to John, his disciple:

> There stood by the cross of Jesus his mother, his mother's sister, Mary of Klopas, and Mary Magdalene. Seeing his mother and the disciple whom he loved standing by her, Jesus said to his mother: "Woman, there is your son!" Then he said to the disciple: "There is your mother!" From that time on the disciple took her to live in his home.

(Jn 19:25-27)

Knowing he was about to die, Jesus looked down from the cross and asked John to love his mother in his place. Because Jesus would not be able to live any longer in this world, he asked that his place with his mother be taken by his disciple. He wanted his mother to continue to be loved as he had loved her.

His mother was a widow, and he was her only son. In accordance with the place of women in society at his time, this meant that Jesus did have a responsibility to see that she would be cared for after his death. He gave her the only inheritance he had to leave with her, his disciples and the love he had awakened in their hearts.

Jesus knew that he also had a responsibility toward the disciples he was leaving behind. They had given up everything to follow him. He had even asked them to give up their family life for him. Now they were to be left. So many had loved him! He had been the center of their lives. Even many of his women disciples had come up to Jerusalem from Galilee to be with him during these holy days. His death would be so sudden! At noon on Thursday he would be among them as always, but by noon the following day he would be already nailed to the cross. A few hours later his body would be placed in the tomb.

That Thursday evening Jesus had anticipated his arrest and death. He knew it was his last supper with them. During the supper he had made it clear that he was leaving them by death, but that his motive in letting himself be taken by his enemies was to obey his Father's will, which was to lay down his life for his followers. They should not think of themselves as abandoned. He was going ahead of them to his Father's house, where he would prepare a lasting place for each of them. There would be plenty of room for everyone! Later, when they also died, he would come back for them, and lead them to the place reserved for them, so that they would be with him and with one another forever (Jn 14:1-3).

Jesus was expressing his great *loyalty* to his new family of brothers and sisters. He had the ability to make such a place for them with him in his own home, just as they had made a home for him in their own hearts. His death would be tragic to them and to him, and it was very painful to leave them, but actually he was proving to them the greatest love any man could have for his friends by dying for them, and then assuring them life in an eternal community with him. He was asking them to trust his loyalty to them.

Trusting his loyalty was what Jesus called having faith. Just as they had faith in God, he said, they should also have faith in him (Jn 14:1). Trusting in Jesus' faithfulness to his disciples became the key to salvation. To believe that he would keep his word and be their savior was the focus of how his followers were to relate to him. In effect, he said: "If you love me, trust me!"

The loyalty of Jesus is also seen by his submission to God's will that he be the fulfillment of the scriptures. As he hung from the cross, he allowed himself to die only when he was sure that his life had fulfilled what the scriptures had promised concerning him (Jn 19:28-30). Included in these promises was that he be God's special gift to Israel. Although his heart opened out to the whole world of nations, he restricted himself to using his gifts and powers for his own people.

It was to his apostles that he entrusted the mission to the Gentiles. When Jesus heard of Greeks wanting to talk with him, he did not think of fleeing with them to escape his impending death, but instead saw this as a sign that he should now be given over to death (Jn 12:20-23), since only then would salvation be offered to all nations.

Not only was Jesus faithful to fulfilling the messianic promises of the scriptures, but he also insisted he was faithful to the Jewish law. He said no one would ever be able to convict him of any sin (Jn 8:46). He had been circumcized according to the law and thereby committed to the Jewish observances. As St. Paul says, Jesus was "born a subject of the law" (Gal 4:4).

## The Accusations against Jesus

When he was brought before the Sanhedrin by his accusers, they could not find any evidence of his having broken any laws, so they had to bring forth false witnesses, who testified that Jesus had said he intended to destroy the Temple, that he opposed paying taxes to Rome, and that he called himself a king. All three of these accusations were a matter of twisting Jesus' words or taking them out of context.

As regards the destruction of the Temple, this Jesus had predicted, but he had never said he himself would do the destroying. In John's gospel, we are told that Jesus was actually referring to his own body as the temple, and that should they destroy his body by killing him he would raise up his body again in three days (Jn 2:21).

As regards the second accusation, we don't have

any evidence that Jesus opposed paying taxes to Rome. Some of his followers were zealots who were eager for an uprising to free Israel from Roman domination, but we do not see Jesus preaching such an uprising. He disappointed many by the fact he was not intent on liberating Israel in that way, and this may have been a reason for some to turn against him, especially Judas. In Jesus' words about rendering to Caesar what is Caesar's (Mk 12:17), Jesus suggested that the image of the emperor on the coins was a sign that by using this money something is owed to the emperor. On the other hand, rendering to God what is God's means we owe something to God when we use what is stamped with his image. This refers directly to the possession of our own existence, since as humans we were created in the image and likeness of God (Gen 1:27).

The third accusation about Jesus calling himself a king was taken up by Pilate. Of course, Jesus could not deny he was the Messiah, if asked, though he often had hidden this from others, even initially from his disciples. In his interrogation of Jesus, Pilate was satisfied Jesus was not claiming to be a political king, and thus was not a threat to the reign of the Roman emperor over Israel. Jesus' kingship had something to do with truth, but Pilate asked: "What is truth?" (Jn 18:38) This might be a philosophical questioning, it might be cynicism about government, or it could imply that truth has no power, especially when compared with military force.

## *Why Was Jesus a Threat?*

Why was Jesus such a threat to the Jewish religious leaders? They had spent their whole lives centered on their religion, just as Jesus had. What made them have such hatred toward him that they did not want him to exist?

They were not necessarily bad men. Jesus said they were *blind,* which can be cited as an excuse for their wrongdoing. Their blindness consisted in not appreciating who Jesus was, how he thought, and what he stood for. We see them being legalistic and self-righteous. They were not seeking to know God in a new way, and certainly not looking for a new religion, even though Jesus had said that his message could not be simply like a new patch on an old garment (Mt 9:16). Somehow their hearts were closed to conversion. All Jesus' followers had had to change their attitudes and behavior in becoming his disciples. The religious leaders, however, had more to lose by such a change of attitudes. After all, the old way of religion benefited them. It brought them authority, wealth, and security.

That the leaders of Israel put to death their own promised Messiah was the greatest irony of religious history. The whole purpose of Israel as chosen people was to bring salvation to all nations through the promised Messiah. They were to keep that hope alive and to live in the expectation of the coming of God's Kingdom. We see them not taking seriously Jesus' claims of messiahship. *They needed him not to be the Messiah.* By having him killed they thought they could prove he was not the Messiah. Thus they watched Jesus on the cross to make sure he died. Perhaps they were so "modern" that they did not believe the scriptures could be fulfilled literally in history. The coming of the Messiah could remain somewhere in their imagination, but would not ever be real in the sense of their actually having to deal with *Him.*

The traditions of Israel in the scriptures were one great divine lesson in being responsible. The genius of Israel's approach to God was that we must be just because God is just. It meant obeying laws. Though they might try to bargain with God as happens within all religions, they knew they received God's blessings by keeping his ordinances. Unfortunately, however, the Jewish religion at that time had become for many a crushing juridicism, which lost sight of God as a Person. Jesus' own experience was that God was not primarily a Lawgiver, but a Father. Jesus died to overcome this false image of God, to free people from what could be described as "a heavy-handed God."

Because of their legalism the Jewish leaders also fell into what we call "self-righteousness." This is a great obstacle to union with God, since by it a person denies the need for repentance or conversion. It is like the placard which reads, "REPENT, AND BE SAVED", where the asterisk leads to a footnote which reads: "If you have already repented, you can disregard this notice." The Jewish leaders, out of self-righteousness, were disregarding the "notice" Jesus was proclaiming. It was Jesus' attack on this self-righteousness and the legalism behind it that made him such a threat, because he was taking away that which gave these leaders their basic security. They thought that the observance of law gave them salvation, or "righteousness," but for Jesus salvation was based instead on the free gift of God we call "grace."

Legalism in religion focuses on the outward observance of laws as assurance that God is pleased with us. We think our relationship with God is based on being obedient to the laws. Instead of being a way in which we honor and love God, the outward observance is made an end in itself. We think we know we are in right relationship with God because we have observed such and such a law, for example, the law of keeping holy the Lord's Day. Out of this legalism, we easily slide into *self-righteousness*. Because we see salvation coming to us, because we have observed the religious laws, any serious *deviance* from such law-keeping takes away our assurance of being saved. As a result, we may be unable to admit to any sin in our lives, for otherwise we would feel very *insecure*. Should someone suggest there is some neglect of obligations on our part, we will have a great need to deny this, or at least respond by pointing out much more serious delinquency in others. Since we think we cannot be *sinners* and still attain salvation, we have to deny we are sinners.

Legalism in religion can also lead us to want to find security by obeying some authority figure. Since it is often difficult to decide what is right or wrong for us to do as we look at abstract laws, we find security by having an external authority make the decision for us. We think that in following the authority figure we will then be on safe ground. Since we were obedient to authority, we conclude that God cannot charge us with doing wrong.

When ultimate security is found in the outward observance of laws, there will be a bias against any changing of the laws. Since right relationship with God is based on the observance of such laws, any talk about changing the laws is reason for anxiety. After all, absolutes are not changeable. Here, again, we see why Jesus was such a threat to the relgious leaders of Israel. He did preach change, and he said the change had to be a whole new way of being religious. The Jewish leaders felt secure with what they knew of their religious obligations. Since the observance of those laws was already a heavy burden, they did not want to hear about any new responsibilities. Any doing away with their existing laws would indicate they were wrong in the past, and that, too, threatened their security.

A contemporary example of this pattern of thinking is when Catholics ask: "What about all those in hell because they ate meat on Friday before the law on Friday abstience was changed?" To answer the question, one must be careful to avoid belittling the past law, but at the same time there is need to show that salvation is not based on outward observance of laws. This can be very confusing to those brought up in the church at a time when great stress was placed on obedience to laws and to all authority.

*Freedom from Slavery to Law*

The gospel as proclaimed by St. Paul states that we are freed from slavery to the law through the death of Jesus on the cross. Paul goes so far as to state that if outward observance of religious laws could assure us of salvation, then "there is no point in the death of Christ" (Gal 2:21). Paul's message on law and grace has always been difficult for christians to comprehend, but it really is worth the effort to do so, since what is at issue is our ultimate security. To build that security on a false base is to invite serious problems in our life. As St. Paul sees it, for Jesus it was worth dying on the cross to give us the true security of salvation through God's grace to replace the old reliance on observing God's laws.

One way to comprehend Paul's interpretation of Jesus' gospel is to distinguish "the spirit of the law" from "the letter of the law". To follow the *spirit* of the law means recognizing that laws are only a *means* to right relationship with God. Following the *letter* of the law, on the other hand, means that laws are an *end* in themselves, where the final arbiter of our relationship with God is observing laws. To St. Paul this would constitute a grave obstacle to my entering into any personal relationship with God at all. We see this in the case of those who conspired against Jesus and brought about his death. They were the Jewish religious leaders, the caretakers of the law who took pride in its observance, and not the tax collectors and prostitutes, who lived outside the law.

The spirit of the law corrects the letter of the law in two ways. First of all, when laws are considered ends in themselves, then all laws tend to have the same importance, since the breaking of any law is an act of disobedience to the lawgiver. Jesus, however, taught that not all laws are equally important. To the scribes and pharisees he spoke of "the weightier matters of the law", which he said were "justice and mercy and faith" (Mt 23:23). He also continually spoke about love of God and neighbor as being the primary commandments on which the whole law depends (Mt 22:38–40).

A second way in which the spirit of the law corrects the letter of the law stems from the fact that obedience to laws does not cause our union with God. As Jesus taught, our union with God is derived from the fact he is our Father. This means that our salvation is based on the grace, or gift, of our divine adoption. Basing our relationship to God on grace, rather than on law, means that we believe God loves us just as we are, because we are his sons and daughters. We are to trust in his promises which come to us through Jesus, and place before him our needs, confident that he wants us to depend on him and on his providence. Such filial union with God as Father causes us to grow also in union with others. This occurs primarily by our trying to imitate God in our attitudes. We are to love others as he loves them, and to listen to their anguish and serve their needs as he does. We are even to express his goodness toward those who hurt us or cause us fear, as Jesus said we should do (Mt 5:44f).

Since the observance of laws honors God and responds to the rights of others, keeping laws is an expression of love for God and neighbor. That is why Jesus said that all the laws and the prophets depend on our loving God and neighbor (Mt 22:40). Learning to love involves learning to relate on a heart level. This is very different from fulfilling laws. On the other hand, we are not talking about simply following a feeling. Love involves a choice to be for the other and to share oneself. It involves confiding and trusting. Since trust is what Jesus was talking about when he asked his disciples to have faith in him, we can conclude that to be united with God through union with Jesus means we have to learn to trust in his goodness toward us. He wants us to love him by trusting his faithfulness to his covenant with us, like a faithful husband wants to be trusted by his wife. Jesus said we can trust him as our Friend as long as we practice his special commandment that we love one another (Jn 15:12-14). Thereby we are keeping our covenant to be recognizable as his disciples. Alongside that concord achieved by sharing our lives, the moral mistakes we commit could be of little significance.

## PASSAGE FOR MEDITATION

I Go to Prepare a Place for You—John 14:1-4.
I Call You Friends—John 15:9-17.
Jesus Before the Sanhedrin—Matthew 28:57-68.
We Are Saved by Faith—Galatians 2:15-21.
Imitate God as His Children—Ephesians 5:1-20.

## QUESTIONS FOR DIALOGUE

1. Where do we see *legalism* in the practise of our religion, and what are its effects?
2. In what way has *self-righteousness* been a problem in our lives?
3. What experience of *security* do we feel because God has adopted us as his sons and daughters?

## SEVEN: His Joviality

Like all SEVENS, Jesus was a *jovial* person. He knew that our Creator intended life is to be enjoyed. Already from the beginning of his ministry, we see him going to parties, such as the wedding reception at Cana:

> And on the third day there was a wedding in Cana of Galilee, and Jesus' mother was there. Both Jesus and his disciples were invited to the wedding.
>
> When they ran out of wine, Jesus' mother said to him: "They don't have any wine."
>
> But Jesus said to her: "Woman, what is that to me and to you? My time has not yet come."
>
> His mother said to the waiters: "Do whatever he says to you."
>
> Now there were six stone water jugs standing there for the Jewish ritual purification, with each one measuring twenty or thirty gallons. Jesus said to them: "Fill the water jugs with water."
>
> So they filled them up to the top. He then said to them: "Dip out some now, and take it to the steward.
>
> So they did that. But when the steward tasted the water which had become wine and did not know where it had come from, — even though the waiters who had dipped out the water knew, — the steward called the bridegroom and said to him: "Everybody puts out the best wine first, and then after people have had plenty to drink he puts out the cheap stuff, but you have kept the best wine until now."
>
> This was the first of Jesus' signs. He did it in Cana of Galilee to manifest his glory, and his disciples believed in him.
>
> (Jn 2:1-11)

The gospel of John chooses to highlight the beginning of Jesus' public ministry with this sign of Jesus' providing wine for a wedding reception. Later Jesus would say that his mission was to bring to people "life in abundance" (Jn 10:10). That abundant life includes a lot of social gatherings.

At Cana Jesus intervened to keep the party going. It was meant to be a sign of the coming of the Kingdom, a fulfillment of messianic abundance. From 120 to 150 gallons of wine is a great amount, and it was of the best vintage. This was like the outpouring of divine love that Jesus was bringing: God's generosity could not be outdone by anyone. Even if we won't be able to experience that love in its fullness until our life in the world to come, we do begin to enjoy it now. Jesus himself enjoyed the anticipation of that eternal party, and he meant the guests at Cana to enjoy it, too. We presume Jesus did not want to be the occasion of a drunken brawl. The wine was to help people have fun together in celebrating the nuptials, rather than get down to serious drinking, which would dampen the fun anyway.

Some religious people, of course, would find it scandalous to encourage such wining and dining, especially on the part of someone claiming to be a prophet from God. One of the first criticisms against Jesus was about such feasting. After the farewell party Matthew threw for his friends to celebrate his becoming a follower of Jesus, some people challenged Jesus about all this eating and drinking. They said John the Baptist and the Pharisees taught their followers to fast. Jesus responded by talking about the need people had to celebrate because he was present with them. He said that as long as he is around people would celebrate, because he was like a bridegroom. When the "bridegroom" was taken away, then people would fast (Mt 9:15). Closeness to Jesus is a special delight to people, so they have to celebrate. Jesus thought such celebration was very appropriate because he did not come to bring sadness. In the course of attending all these banquets Jesus gained a reputation of enjoying wine. He was comfortable while at parties with people, and was not ill at ease or yearning to get away to his prayers or study, or even to a more austere diet.

Then there was the occasion when Jesus himself threw a beach party. The event occurred after his resurrection. The apostles, led by Peter, were really supposed to be doing missionary work, but instead they decided to go fishing. It was a stag party, and the fact they caught nothing all night probably did not spoil their fun very much. As the sun was rising they saw the figure of a man on shore who called out: "Boys, have you caught anything?" (Jn 21:5). They had to say no. He told them to throw out their nets on the port side. Supposing the stranger saw something they didn't see, they obeyed him, and at once the nets were almost tearing apart because they were so filled with fish. John whispered to Peter: "It's the Lord!" (Jn 21:7). There Peter was without a stitch of clothing on. He threw on his robe and jumped into the water to splash ashore. That must have looked very funny to everyone, especially to Jesus. Evidently Peter was torn between covering up and being excited about seeing the Lord. Jesus, however, did not make any fuss or scold them in any way for slacking off from being apostles. He joined in their fun by inviting them to breakfast. He had bread and had a fish cooking on the grill over a charcoal fire. He told them to get some of their own fish to cook, too. Peter went to the boat, which had been anchored along the shoreline, and dragged the net full of fish onto the beach. Peter proceeded to count them, to a total of 153 big fish. This would be a fish story fascinating to audiences of early christians whenever some of the apostles came to talk about the experiences they had had with Jesus.

This sign of messianic abundance of food was also experienced in Jesus' multiplication of loaves and fish in the desert (Mk 6:35-44;8:1-10), stories which have eucharistic connotations. Later Jesus wanted his disciples to see the meaning of there having been many baskets of leftovers (Mk 8:19-21). To have forgotten to bring enough provisions was to be no cause for worry because of our faith in God's care of us, which not only provides enough, but often an abundance. Jesus also pointed to this abundance by changing bread and wine into his body and blood at the last supper, as a sign of what his death would bring to us. As his followers we are to enjoy a never-ending nourishment from the human presence of Jesus until the end of time, and this will ensure us of the joy of eternal life (Jn 6:54).

We see in Jesus' heart always the expectation of good times to come because of the promised Kingdom. He sees great importance in telling everyone that God intends us to enjoy life forever as a community, which in many ways will be like an everlasting wedding feast. Community celebration became the principal way of christian worship in memory of Jesus' death. The pre-christian worship of destroying something in order to place it ritually in God's hands was replaced by celebrating a ritual meal around a table. In later ages there was a tendency of christians to take away the party and make worship much more ascetic and sacrificial, with stone altars replacing dining-room tables, and kneelers replacing chairs. The tradition of everyone present drinking from the cup dropped out of favor, and instead of breaking a loaf of bread to be shared among all, separate wafers were substituted with an unappealing taste. Often the wine used was bitter,—perhaps to keep the sacristan from sipping some on the side,—and no one thought anything wrong in consecrating stale hosts instead of fresh. It even became customary that the laity would not receive communion more than once or twice a year. Instead they would recite prayers of "spiritual communion", and revere the consecrated bread by placing it in a monstrance. No wonder we needed a liturgical movement to ask the question: "What happened to the community celebration?"

Why shouldn't eucharistic liturgy mean "having a good time"? It can be if we return to Jesus' attitude toward the sign of messianic abundance, and the message that the Kingdom of God means the union of people around one table. When we think of God as a strict Lawgiver and heavy-handed Judge, we tend to see worship fulfilling a law by giving up something for God. Since worship is described as a "sacrifice," we think it must involve some kind of loss, which connotes sadness and a burden. There is another notion of sacrifice, however, and this is one that is very faithful to christian tradition as enunciated already by St. Augustine. Here sacrifice means *whatever serves to unite us with God.* Since God wants us to become united with him personally, sacrifice will be some kind of personal sharing. Persons are united by mutual sharing of themselves. God shares his love with us by what we receive in the eucharist, and we respond with a joyous celebration of thanks. Celebration is most typified by a nuptial feast, and that is a model for christian worship. Perhaps we need to avoid talking about sacrifice, and go back to the word eucharist, which in Greek means "thanksgiving". It is by celebration that we worship God in the best way, because we are filled with joy by sharing together his special gifts to his messianic people.

## The Mistake of Living Only for Fun

The preceding can be very well appreciated by SEVENS, who think life should be one big party anyway. Their shadow side comes into play, however, when they want to cover up all the hardships in life and avoid all that is painful or burdensome. Probably they had a warm, cozy childhood, and after becoming adults still want everything to be enjoyable. They don't like any situation to get too serious, and when they feel it does they intervene by telling anecdotes or suggesting that everyone go out for ice cream. They think that we should somehow find fun in everything we do.

As a result, any kind of pain becomes a very great evil to be avoided. We see this in the tendency of SEVENS to procrastination. It is fun to make plans, but generally the implementation is tedious, and so they put it off, much to the disappointment of those counting on them to do their part. Indeed, any kind of discipline, even that of keeping on a topic at a meeting, is in some sense painful, and so they want to shirk it. All this is done for the value of making life

enjoyable for everyone. SEVENS tend to overindul-
gence in eating and drinking because they want to
enjoy life. Often a man who is a SEVEN chooses a
wife who is a ONE or a SIX. His good nature is
attractive to such a woman, who needs someone to
help her have a good time. As a SEVEN, however, he
tends to lack a sense of intimacy. He also likes to be
the "eternal boy", and lets his wife take care of the
bills, and also do all the worrying about the diet he is
supposed to follow. She lives to a ripe, old age, but in
widowhood, for he dies in his middle years from the
effects of being overweight.

## Accepting Trials and Afflictions

By always seeking to enjoy life SEVENS want to
overlook the pain others are suffering. They could
find themselves in a position like that of the rich
man, who according to Jesus' parable feasted sumptu-
ously every day, while overlooking the poor man at
his gate (Lk 16:19ff). There is a great deal of injustice
in the world. To fail to see the poverty and oppression caused by this injustice is to miss the very reason
Jesus came. One area of oppression comes from ethnic
discrimination. All his life Jesus and his family suffered
in some way from the domination of the Romans
over Israel. This came to the forefront for Jesus when
the Roman procurator, Pontius Pilate, handed Jesus
over to the palace guard to be scourged (Mk 15:15-19).
Because it was being said that Jesus claimed to be the
Messiah,—the promised King of the Jews,—the Roman
soldiers saw their opportunity to express their anti-
Semitism. Mocking him with a purple robe and a

crown of thorns, they spat on him to show how they despised all Jews. Pilate, too, mocked the Jewish leaders by asking them if they wanted their king to be nailed to the cross (Jn 19:15). Had Jesus been a fellow Roman, Pilate would never have condemned him to death. Being aware that the Romans were using him as an object of their anti-Semitism, Jesus told the women of Jerusalem who were weeping for him as he carried his cross that they should weep for themselves and for their children (Lk 23:28). He indicated that this suffering of his was only the beginning of the persecution the Romans would heap on the Jews in their capital city. His words about the green and dry wood (Lk 23:31) meant that if they do this now to him when the city is quiet, what will they do when the people become rebellious?

Not only could the craving to have life always full of fun cause SEVENS to overlook injustice in the world, but it could also cause them to seek a false security in pleasures. Jesus indicated that to be existentially secure we need to accept the trials of life. To try to escape pain may deprive us of real joy in the end. There is a price to pay for what is good. Jesus liked to compare the labor pains of a mother with the pains his followers would suffer because of him. He said that when the time of labor begins the mother is sad because of the suffering involved, but once her child is born she forgets the pain she endured because she has brought a child into the world (Jn 16:21). Jesus compared his own passion and death to a seed being planted. He said that unless the seed dies it remains alone, but if it dies it produces many grains (Jn 12:24). Paul's letters are also filled with exhortations that we accept discipline and other hardships in our life so that we may attain what is good. As Timothy is told, "we work hard and struggle because we have set our hope on the living God . . . " (1 Tim 4:10). To the Romans St. Paul wrote of rejoicing in our sufferings, "knowing that affliction brings about patience, and patience builds character, which in turn gives us hope . . . " (Rm 5:4f).

One of the clearest presentations of living the paschal mystery in our time is formulated by creation-centered spirituality, especially as outlined in *Original Blessings* by Matthew Fox.[1] Our spirituality is to begin with the enjoyment of life, accepting in gratitude all the good we discover around us (*Via Positiva*). Not to appreciate the good of creation is to fail to appreciate the divine Creator. A day arrives, however, when trials come which take away some of the good we have possessed (*Via Negativa*). These trials are a time of grace, calling for us to "let go", and entrust ourselves into the hands of God, like Job did when he said to his wife: "The Lord gave, and now he has taken away. May his name be praised!" (Job 1:21). Out of this acceptance of *loss* the grace of God can engender within us a new creativity, like a kind of resurrection (*Via Creativa*). Through the development and exercise of this new creativity with others we can be an instrument of God for the transformation of the world (*Via Transformativa*).

That transformation of the world into the Kingdom of God was depicted by Old Testament prophets

---

[1]Matthew Fox, *Original Blessing,* Bear & Co., Santa Fe, New Mexico, 1983.

as God's dream for the world. It was to be a great banquet for all the nations. God will send out messengers to each nation to call each people to come to God's holy mountain and there place before God all the riches of their own culture. Then God will bless each nation and invite its people to sit down with all the other nations at a table prepared by God himself. During this great banquet God will settle all the disputes between the nations. Then all the nations will decide to melt down their weapons of war and use the metal to manufacture farm implements. An everlasting covenant of peace will be concluded so that "nations will never again go to war, never prepare for battle again" (Is 2:4).

## PASSAGES FOR MEDITATION

The Question about Fasting—Matthew 9:14-17.
Jesus' Appears on the Shore of Tiberias—John 21:1-13.
Jesus Feeds the Crowd of Five Thousand—Mark 6:30-44.
Jesus the Bread of Life—John 6:25-59.
Jesus Accepts Death Like a Grain of Wheat—John 12:20-33.
The Vision of Everlasting Peace—Isaiah 2:1-4.

## QUESTIONS FOR DIALOGUE

1. How have I experienced Jesus making my plans turn out even better than I expected?
2. Who are some persons we know who are especially light-hearted and fun-loving? What makes them that way?

3. How have I found it to be true in my life that pain
   is not necessarily to be avoided? What good has
   come out of some of the pain I have endured?

## EIGHT: His Assertiveness

EIGHTS take pride in being *strong persons.* The stories in the bible are filled with such heroes. Already in the Old Testament the Spirit of God provided prophets and kings with extraordinary strength. We think of the boy David facing the mighty Goliath with a slingshot, and of Judith all alone in the enemy camp wielding the sword of General Holofernes. In the New Testament we see Paul being stoned, and then getting up, brushing himself off, and returning to the city. Most of all, of course, we see Jesus as a strong person.

Every christian child knows of this strength of Jesus in his chasing out the money-changers from the Temple, which according to John's gospel occurred early in his public life:

> As the Passover of the Jews drew near, Jesus went up to Jerusalem. He found in the Temple vendors of oxen, sheep, and doves, with the moneychangers seated nearby. He made a whip out of rope and drove all the sheep and oxen out of the Temple. He scattered the coins of the moneychangers and overturned their tables. To those selling doves he said: "Take these things out of here; don't make the house of my Father a house of merchandise".
>
> His disciples remembered that it was written of him: "Zeal for your house will consume me."
>
> (Jn 2:13–17)

With his strong sense of reverence for God, Jesus decided to confront head-on the disgrace of commercialism in the sacred precincts of the Temple at Jerusalem. Probably as a boy he had already been shocked by it, and thus it is likely that he could have done this at his first visit to Jerusalem after his baptism.

That he was able so readily to disperse the merchants and their animals suggests that these vendors knew they were in the wrong. It was, of course, what a prophet would do. The disciples, however, seem to have been surprised, probably because of the anger Jesus displayed. They later explained this aggressiveness in Jesus as a fulfillment of the scriptures. It was zeal for his Father's house that burned in him.

Another prominent example from the gospels which displayed Jesus' prophetic confrontation of official injustice is seen in Jesus' stern preaching against the hypocrisy of the scribes and Pharisees (Mt 23:13–36). They said he had insulted them. He certainly did not mince any words as he charged them with being "hypocrites" (v. 15), "blind guides" (v. 16), "whitewashed tombs" (v. 27), and "snakes, the offspring of vipers" (v. 33). Jesus did not hesitate to take on the whole religious establishment. He was motivated in his attack by his great distaste for people playing roles and pretending to be holy and just. They were in a place of image-setting for the whole country on what God was like and what God willed, yet they used their wealth and education for their own self-interest. They were conspiring to get rid of Jesus, whom they correctly saw as a threat to all they had attained. Jesus continually sought to become their savior by leading them to repentance. His tactic was to be strong with the strong, and to keep telling them they were *blind.* On their part these religious professionals even went to the extent of bribing one of Jesus' disciples in order to get him arrested, they called on false witnesses in his trial in order to have him convicted, and after angels opened his tomb while soldiers were guarding it, they bribed the soldiers to say that Jesus' disciples stole the body while the soldiers were sleeping (Mt 28:12f).

These men were not only blind; they were malicious and seemed not even to fear God himself. As part of the wealthy class in Israel, they made an alliance with their Roman conquerers in order to crucify Jesus. They saw Jesus as stirring up the people in a way that jeopardized their own cozy position, which they saw as depending on keeping the *status-quo*. The Romans were only too ready to oblige, even though Pilate saw Jesus as no threat to continued Roman domination.

Jesus did not remain silent about the evil he saw in his society just because he did not have any political power to do much about it, or because he might be killed,—as indeed he was. He firmly believed that the people responsible for injustice should be told so to their faces; otherwise they would be blind to their sinfulness and keep on oppressing others for their own advantage. To let the injustice remain hidden was to play into the hands of those who conspire to evil. As St. Paul says, the children of the light are to bring all things to light (Eph 5:11ff). Those who conspire to evil hate the light and flee from it, for once their injustice is exposed they lose much of their power, since it depends on deception.

Jesus thus is a model for all persons with a strong sense of justice and a readiness to challenge the establishment. Such persons see, as Jesus did, that those who use violence to defend their positions or make their power felt by others are really acting out of weakness. True strength is seen in those who, as

Jesus says, do not fear those who can kill the body but cannot dispose of the soul (Mt 10:28). As his followers, we are not to compromise our convictions, even if we have to suffer for them.

## Strong But Not Cantankerous

It is very noble to be always ready to confront injustice, but it is not noble to be always trying to pick a fight. Behind such cantankerousness may be the exhilaration of one's own self-assertion. EIGHTS want to make others deal with them, especially those with power and authority. They enjoy having it out with people, and have a skill in picking out weaknesses in others, especially the skeletons in their closets, i.e., their hidden and shameful wrongdoings. EIGHTS often feel justified to use such tactics to unmask the pretenses of the powerful, and bring to light what many suspect, namely, that those in power are there for selfish reasons. EIGHTS are often difficult to relate to, because they tend to step on the toes of others, and even take over the turf of others, all without any sense of wrongdoing. They consider they are being good persons by being strong persons. EIGHTS consider that anyone who has difficulty with their assertiveness has to deal with that as his or her own problem.

In trying to understand this shadow typical of EIGHTS, it is helpful to see that aggressiveness often comes out of an inner insecurity. After all, one good way of defending the self is to intimidate others. Inner fears thus are the origin of outer aggressivity. This itself is deceiving, of course, since this assertiveness seems to portray fearlessness, and the EIGHT may think that is so. Once others catch on, however, that the EIGHT is being aggressive because of inner fears, they have an insight on how to help. One way is to be very strong and direct, to show the EIGHT you are not afraid of him or her. The other way is to try to do whatever will increase his or her *security,* since it is insecurity that is causing the aggressiveness. EIGHTS especially need help to discover love. They may never have learned how to relate in love, since that entails *submission* to others. It probably would come as a great surprise to many EIGHTS that love often is expressed by *giving in* to another.

## Being Vulnerable

Despite the strength of his personality, Jesus often reacted to the sinful behavior of others by gentleness rather than by confrontation. He defended the adulterous woman from condemnation (Jn 8:10f), invited himself to the house of a notorious tax collector named Zachaeus (Lk 19:5), and avoided following John the Baptist's challenge to King Herod's adulterous life (Lk 3:19). It wasn't in Jesus' strategy to confront injustice wherever it was. He warned his followers not to take on a losing battle (Lk 14:31f); they needed to be prudent like snakes, and not only innocent like doves (Mt 10:16). He got the reputation of fraternizing with a lot of sinful types, many of whom were justifiably excommunicated from the synagogue. To those who complained about this he said that he had come not for the just but for sinners (Mk 2:17).

We can also say that despite his public attack on

the scribes and Pharisees, he avoided denouncing
them as individuals. Perhaps this came from his understanding that many people become trapped in their
self-interest as a class or economic group. He attacked
the self-interest and even maliciousness of the Jewish
religious leaders without necessarily putting down
any individual scribe or pharisee. After all, we find
Jesus on occasion being invited to eat at a pharisee's
house (Cf Lk 7:36), and his night visitor, Nicodemus,
was also a pharisee (Jn 3:1).

More important is the fact that we will never understand the prophetic stance of Jesus unless we see his
willingness to be *vulnerable*. St. Paul says that in
becoming man the Son of God emptied himself and
took on weakness as the condition of being human
(Phil 2:7). Jesus especially showed his weakness
through his passion and death. It was through that
weakness that our salvation was brought about, just
as his mother had spoken of the humiliation of her
pregnancy being used by God to lift up the poor (Lk
1:46ff). Jesus voluntarily allowed himself to be weak,
as is shown by his telling his disciples that he had the
power to prevent his arrest (Mt 26:53). In giving
himself up voluntarily he was going to be simply a
human being and not call on divine power to protect
himself. When the soldiers came to arrest Jesus, he
stood up before them and asked: "Who are you looking
for?" When they said, "Jesus of Nazareth", he replied,
"I am he", and at once they fell to the ground (Jn
18:4-6). Despite the weapons they had in their hands,
they were still afraid of Jesus. There he stood before
them without any weapons of defense, but utterly
fearless, and with his reputation as a man of God and

a miracle worker. His voice itself was enough to bring them to their knees. Jesus was in control of the situation even then. He told them to let his disciples go (Jn 18:8), and only then did he allow them to take him prisoner. Peter made a wild attempt in defense by cutting off the ear of a slave named Malchus. Jesus rebuked him and said: "Whoever takes up the sword will die by the sword" (Mt 26:52). Even though Jesus died anyway, he was making a point about violence which his followers today are still struggling to understand.

As his mother had expressed it in her Magnificat, Jesus saw that God would work through human weakness, and especially through his own. As he had earlier said to those who were hostile to him: "If you destroy this temple I will raise it up in three days" (Jn 2:19). They were given power to destroy his body, but he had power to raise it from the dead. He also had said that he would be lifted up on a pole so that all human beings could look up to him to be healed of their sins (Jn 3:14). Seeing him naked and weak and bloody, and utterly powerless, their hearts would be moved to repent. At the moment of his death on Calvary there were already those who were touched. The centurion cried out that they had killed an innocent man" (Lk 23:47). On Pentecost, when Peter preached to them, many others saw that they had put to death the one sent to them by God, and their hearts were opened to the gospel (Acts 2:37–42). As Jesus had predicted, his death on the cross would accomplish what otherwise he had been unable to do, namely, to convert the Jewish leaders.

Had Jesus defended himself with violent means

and thereby thwarted their conspiracy to put him to death, they would have continued to maintain they were right. Just because another is superior through the use of force does not convince us we are wrong-doers. Jesus was concerned about converting. You don't convert by violence, no matter how right you are. Jesus' disciples are to be witnesses of truth, justice and peace, but these cannot be protected and promoted by what contradicts them, such as deception, injustice, and violence. It is strange any christians could have thought otherwise. Our way of dealing with the sin of the world is to be willing to die for gospel values, confident that the stance of nonviolence is God's way of overcoming evil and oppression.

## *The Power of Martyrdom*

One common argument against non-violence is that it does not work. Jesus showed it does, and he meant this as a lesson for his disciples in the future. Destroying one's enemies does not build God's Kingdom; converting them does. To do that, their hearts have to be touched. They are blinded by their self-righteousness. To get them to see differently they need to discover that they are being seriously unjust to others. Whenever the oppressed take up a violent means of defense, their oppressors feel justified in using force to put down the uprising. It is by speaking the truth about the injustice and then being willing to suffer for what one has said that the tremendous power of *martyrdom* can begin to operate on earth to bring about abiding justice. This willingness to suffer even death when one speaks out comes from the conviction of divine backing. To achieve justice in God's way renders useless all the so-called power the oppressors have. They cannot bribe with their money, nor can they coerce by the threat of death. Even if their hearts are not touched, and they remain in the darkness of their sin, they will have to see the inner power of the christian martyr who is willing to die for the truth.

All too often christians extolled martyrs because they were promised a heavenly reward, while at the same time many so-called christian nations glorified military power and war. Children were told stories of great heroes who gave their lives for their country, as though one's nation was God's Kingdom. Hardly anyone spoke of touching the enemy's heart with the grace of conversion, yet that is what christian witness is supposed to be about. The Holy Spirit promised by Jesus to his followers is to *convince* the world of its injustice (Jn 16:8).

We are not in this world to *earn* heaven. We already have that awaiting us. We are put here and given faith and membership in Christ's Body in order to be instruments for God's plan of overcoming the sin of the world. He intends to do that through our witness. Somewhere, sometime, christians are obliged to take a stand against injustice. It is to be done in a non-violent way, for our truth needs to bring life to the world and not more death. Satan rules by the force of death; God's Kingdom rules by truth, and that truth can bring us freedom (Gal 5:1).

It is by being closely united in Christ that we can become fearless in speaking out, while at the same time being willing to suffer for the truth without resorting to counter-violence. Jesus' teachings on non-violence still remain very controversial among his followers as we ponder the traditional use of violence in order to achieve justice and peace within our own nation and between all nations. The question is, do we confront evil in ways that can lead others to see their injustice and thereby repent, or do we simply want to *prevail* over all who do wrong?

The futility of past ways of defending the christian faith through violence is illustrated by Garrison Keillor in his best seller, *Lake Wobegon Days,* as he recalls how he, as a Protestant boy, thought about Catholics as he watched their parish parade on Memorial Day:

> . . . I turn to see the Catholics swing out onto Taft (Street) and head for our rear. Our numbers are approximately equal, but if they attacked, they would rout us in a minute. I've read *Foxx's Book of Martyrs,* and it's hard to forget: scenes of faithful Huguenot believers praying quietly and praising God and forgiving the hordes of Catholics who pile kindling at their feet. If the Knights were to tie me to a telephone pole and pile dry brush around me and call on me to renounce my faith while a Catholic Boy Scout prepares his flints, what would I do then? I guess I'd renounce, all right. Kiss a statue, hold a crucifix, do what they said. I could always cross my fingers at the time and prevent a real conversion. God would know I didn't mean it.[1]

## PASSAGES FOR MEDITATION

Jesus Confronts the Scribes and Pharisees—Matthew 23:13-36.
The Promise of the Spirit—John 15:18-16:15.
The Arrest of Jesus—John 18:1-11.

---

[1]Garrison Keillor, *Lake Wobegon Days,* Viking, New York, 1985, p. 119.

Peter's Pentecost Sermon—Acts 2:14-39.
Christ's Humility and Greatness—Phillipians 2:5-11.

## QUESTIONS FOR DIALOGUE

1. What do I especially admire in the way Jesus confronts people? How do I see him as a model for my own self-assertion?
2. Where do I see people being *hypocrites?* How do I feel about the way they are?
3. How did Jesus teach an attitude of non-violent witness of the truth, and how do we try to live that out in our lives today as his followers?

## NINE: His Serenity

Jesus was a man of great tranquility. Especially in these days when many people are experiencing great turmoil and insecurity in life, we need to know his serenity and peacefulness. Although life for him during his public ministry was often like being at war,—as sometimes seems true also in our lives,—he did carry within himself the deep peace of the Holy Spirit. He wanted his disciples to share his peace (Jn 14:27), and said people should come to him in order to find rest in their souls (Mt 11:29). When the disciples, most of whom were seasoned fishermen, became panicstricken because a sudden storm on the lake threatened to capsize their fishing boat, Jesus remained asleep with his head on a cushion (Mk 4:35ff). When they woke him because of the danger, he chided them for being persons of "little faith", and then told the winds and the waves to be still. Suddenly there was a "great calm".

On a later occasion when the disciples were alone on the lake late at night and saw Jesus walking toward them on the waves, they screamed in fear because they thought he was a ghost (Mt 14:25ff). Jesus shouted to them that it was he and so they should not be afraid. When he invited Peter to walk out on the lake to join him, Peter tried but was overcome again with great fear and as he began to sink he shouted for help. Jesus caught him by the hand, said he had "little faith", and asked why he had doubted. As soon as they got into the boat the wind suddenly died down. We thus see Jesus trying to teach his disciples that because he is with them they should be peaceful even when they are struck by sudden storms.

It is especially as risen Lord that Jesus communicated his deep serenity to his followers. Because he now had attained a new peacefulness from his triumph over the powers of death, there was something so different about his bearing that his followers initially failed to recognize him when he appeared to them. To study this serenity in the risen Jesus let us begin with his first apparition as recorded by St. John's gospel, that of his appearance to Mary Magdalene at the tomb on Easter Sunday morning:

> Mary, however, stood crying just outside the tomb. As she was crying she stooped down into the tomb and saw two angels in white sitting where the body of Jesus had lain, with one at the head and the other at the feet.
> These said to her: "Woman, why are you crying?"
> She said to them: "They took my Lord and I don't know where they put him." Having said this she turned around and saw Jesus standing, but did not know that it was Jesus.
> Jesus said to her: "Woman, why are you crying? Whom are you seeking?"
> Thinking it is the gardener, she said to him: "Sir, if you carried him away, tell me where you put him and I will go and get him."
> Jesus said to her: "Mary!"
> She turned to him and said to him in Hebrew: "Rabboni!" (which means "Teacher").
> Jesus said to her: "Don't keep holding on to me, because I have not yet ascended to the Father, but go to my brothers and sisters and say to them: 'I am ascending to my Father and your Father, to my God and your God.' "
> Mary Magdalene came and announced to the disciples: "I have seen the Lord, and he said these things to me."
> (Jn 20:11-18)

Just before dawn that Easter morning, Mary Magdalene had been running through the streets of Jerusalem (Jn 20:1-10). She got Peter and John out of bed to come to the empty tomb. They investigated the tomb and then left, with Peter especially being bewildered by the missing body of Jesus. Mary remained next to the open tomb. She stooped down to look in and saw two angels in white. They asked her why she was in tears. After answering, she backed out of the tomb. A man standing nearby asked her why she was in tears, using the same words as the angels had used. She responded without looking at him. Mary was utterly torn up by the thought that someone had handled the Lord's body and carried it off. When she heard the man call her name, she suddenly realized he was Jesus. She turned toward him and with great joy threw her arms around him. Having found him again, she was not going to let him go. Jesus, however, said to her that she must not keep holding on to him. What did he mean? It is not that he did not want to be touched, for later that same day at his appearance to the disciples in the upper room he would tell them to touch him to prove he was not a ghost (Lk 24:39). What Jesus was telling Mary Magdalene is that she was not to cling to this appearance of him. Mary Magdalene thought Jesus was simply alive again, and that she would be able to follow him as she had done before his death. He was not simply alive again, however; he was now the risen Lord, and hence he would not normally be visible any more. What she was experiencing was an appearance of him to show her he was present. In the future she would need to learn how to recognize his presence without such appearances.

Later that same day, two disciples were making their way home to Emmaus (Lk 24:13-35). They had left the community of disciples in Jerusalem because

Jesus had been killed. To them this meant he was not the Messiah after all. Their faith in him had been shattered. Very downhearted, they were returning to their home to pick up their old lives again. As they were walking along they came upon a stranger, who then walked with them. He asked what they had been talking about on the road. They stopped, and with sad faces told him about having followed Jesus of Nazareth as the one they had thought was going to fulfill God's promises to his people, but then he had been killed. The stranger responded by saying that the fact that Jesus had been killed was no reason to stop believing in him as the promised Messiah. He cited for them many texts from the scriptures which had predicted that the Messiah would indeed be rejected by the people and put to death, but that then he would rise to his glory.

When they reached their town the stranger indicated that he had to go on, but they urged him to come in and stay with them, because, as they said, it was already late in the day. He came in and reclined with them at table over supper. He took the bread, said the blessing, broke the bread and handed it to them. At that moment they recognized he was really Jesus, but as soon as they recognized him he faded out of sight. They rushed back to Jerusalem and pounded on the locked door of the house where they had had the last supper. After they were admitted and began telling the others what had happened, they turned around and there was Jesus again. He had not entered through the door. It had remained locked. He was appearing to show them he had been there all the time in their midst.

The apostle Thomas had not been there. Later the disciples excitedly told Thomas that Jesus had appeared to them as risen from the dead (Jn 20:24f). Thomas replied that he would not believe unless he could put his fingers into the holes the nails had made in Jesus' hands, and place his hand in the opening the spear had made in his side. We speak of "doubting Thomas", but he was also "pouting Thomas." He felt left out. Wasn't he just as good as the other apostles? Why had not Jesus appeared to him? The problem was not that Thomas was less loved by Jesus, but rather that he had not been with the community, and it is to the community that the risen Jesus came. As Jesus had promised, he would be present wherever two or three of his disciples gathered in his name (Mt 18:20).

The next Sunday Thomas was with the community of the disciples in the upper room, and again Jesus appeared in their midst (Jn 20:26–29). He took Thomas aside, and Thomas made an act of faith. Jesus said to him that it was fine that he believed because he had seen, but more blessed were those who believe without having seen. What is it that we believe without having seen? Not simply that Jesus is risen from the dead, but that he comes to be with us when we gather in his name. This we call the *communitarian presence of Jesus.*

We may ask what difference does it make that the risen Jesus should be present when christians gather together. After all, God is present everywhere. Here, however, we are not talking about the omnipresence of God, but about the presence of the living Jesus, who once walked this earth, was nailed to the cross, and now lives as risen Lord. It is he who comes to be with us when we form bonds with one another. To "gather in his name" means that we form bonds together as his followers in obedience to his commandment that we love one another as he has loved us (Jn 13:34f). The effect of this presence is a special experience in which Jesus joins our gathering to help us be a community.

The resurrection appearances indicated some of what we experience from his presence in our christian community. First of all, he opens hearts to the meaning of the scriptures. He did this, for example, on the road to Emmaus (Lk 24:27), and again at his meeting with his disciples later that day in the upper room (Lk 24:45). Through this they were able to interpret what was currently happening in their lives in the light of the scriptures. It made God's word in the bible practical, bringing them serenity of mind in the midst of problems and hardships.

The presence of the risen Jesus in their gathering also gave them a new feeling. When he was with them they were filled with joy, and as the disciples had reflected on their walk with Jesus to Emmaus, they remembered the feeling they had had of a burning in their hearts (Lk 24:32). The risen Jesus came to share with them his *peace* to allay their fears and worries.

## Avoiding Indolence

Sometimes people who have a great deal of serenity in their lives don't have much *action*. NINES tend to be very content with life as it is, and take pains to avoid whatever might upset their complacency. This means avoiding all conflicts and tensions, and taking pride in being "easy-going". NINES like routine, and don't want to be disturbed from their accustomed daily life. They are comfortable with old friends and are little interested in making new ones. They like pastimes such as watching TV, playing cards, following sports, and collecting knicknacks.

Something of this indolent complacency is suggested to us by the seven apostles who went out fishing instead of getting busy becoming missionaries (Jn 21:2ff). Camaraderie is wonderful, but that is not exactly what Jesus had in mind when he came to be with his disciples as risen Lord. When he went aside with Peter that morning after their having had breakfast on the beach, he asked Peter if he loved him with the love of *agápe,* which is God's way of loving (Jn 21:15ff). Peter's answer was that Jesus knew he loved him with the love of *philía,* which is the love of friendship. Jesus wanted Peter to see that life with him is not to be comfortable or easy. Out of love for Jesus Peter was to have pastoral care for the community of disciples, over those whom Jesus called his flock. To do that Peter could not let the group of apostles just be a camaraderie of hail-fellow-well-met, and be taking off his clothes as he fishes with them. He had to go out to both women and men and draw them all together into the communion of God's new family. There is going to be some tension in doing that, and a lot of hard work. In particular, God's kind of love involves taking *initiative.*

Because they want life without conflict, NINES often fail to act with the kind of love that takes initiative. This may be due to a poor self-image. Those who think they are not worth much probably won't do much. They may think that whatever they accomplish is not worth a hill of beans anyway. The problem is, however, that if they don't make much happen they will end up feeling they are not worth much. Such lack of self-esteem probably has roots in their childhood. Maybe their parents fought a lot, and as children they craved for a home without conflict. They became *resigned* to not feeling much love from their parents and said it really did not matter. They ended up with the attitude that not much happens in life, anyway, and so there isn't anything that is really worth getting excited about. As a consequence, NINES make their lives a routine without clear priorities. They take life as it comes, but try to avoid whatever gets in the way of their "peace." This sounds, however, very much like the peace that the world has to give rather than the peace that Jesus gives (Jn 14:27). He came, after all, to make life different, and since his resurrection he intends to do this through the actions of his followers. This would happen, he said, once they were empowered from on high by the Holy Spirit.

## The Promised Power from Above

Despite all the giftedness of the presence of the risen Jesus with the community of his disciples, he knew that something more was needed for them to continue his ministry. The peacefulness of community was a great gift, but more was needed for the great task of building God's Kingdom among all nations. This was especially true of those who were looking for community only because of their own need.

As risen Jesus he wanted to bring to his disciples a new energy. By his appearances he commissioned his disciples to go out to meet people, and to bear witness of him even before those who would be hostile. Initially as disciples they "learned" from him. Then they became apostles who were "sent" to others. As risen Lord he promised to be with them all days, even to the end of the world (Mt 28:20). He wanted to give them confidence, and even a fearlessness, which would grow out of the conviction that his Spirit would assist them as they spoke (Mt 10:19f). This third divine Person who had been with Jesus would come to be with them also, and then they would be empowered to be his pastoral ministers and witnesses to the end of the earth.

This gift of the Spirit is given so that each of us receives a part of the gifts and powers which Jesus himself received when the Holy Spirit came down upon him at his baptism. Like Jesus, we too have God as our Father, and the Spirit gives us an inner sense of being God's adopted sons and daughters (Gal 4:6). By sending to each of us a share in Jesus' own powers, the Father is saying to us that he believes in us,—that he believes we will develop and use our spiritual gift for the upbuilding of his Kingdom.

In order to use our spiritual gift, however, we need to pool it with those received by our fellow christians. St. Paul described this as our becoming the Body of Christ (1 Cor 12:12ff). Each individual in the christian community is like one organ of the human body, such as an eye, an ear, a hand, or a foot. Each part is different because each has a special power or function. The eye can see, the ear can hear, hands can handle, and feet can walk. One organ is not really able to substitute for another, and each needs the others. So it is in the christian community. I have a unique gift from God, one that others do not have, and by all of us working together in harmony we will be able to make the whole of Jesus' powers effective in our world in a way that will transform it.

Obviously, as part of the Body of Christ, I am accountable for using my gifts. Others are not to replace me. I should be grateful to be needed, and to be part of the whole community on mission. The greatest gift I have, though, is that of love (1 Cor 13:13). That is the gift of myself to the others and my welcoming them into my life. I am to know that I am able to love with Jesus' own love, and like Peter I am called not just to enjoy friendship but to care for the harmony and unity of all, that we be brothers and sisters in one family, living a shared life in a shared world. To be able to love, of course, I must first of all be loved. It is the power of mutual love expressed in the christian community which can awaken me to my great worth as God's gift to others. This gift of mutual love is what my heart has always been longing for. It is experienced, however, only by my own gift of myself, and by being willing to be responsible in creating community life as well as in sharing it.

NINES need to be called into community. They are looking for outside stimulation to find more life and energy. They will respond when they are invited to take part, especially by those who truly believe in them and their gift. They are grateful to be considered SOMEBODY, and ordinarily will make excellent community members, much concerned for the spirit of harmony among all. They do need to be held accountable, that they see no one else can replace them and that they become convinced their contribution makes a difference to others.

## PASSAGES FOR MEDITATION

Jesus Calms a Storm — Mark 4:35-41.
Jesus Walks on Water — Matthew 14:22-33.
The Walk to Emmaus — Luke 24:13-35.
The Risen Jesus with Thomas — John 20:24-29.
The Risen Jesus with Peter — John 21:15-19.
One Body of Christ with Many Parts — 1 Corinthians 12:12-31.

## QUESTIONS FOR DIALOGUE

1. Who are some very calm and peaceful people we know? What makes them that way?
2. Where do we see persons who are "burned out", and really lacking in energy and enthusiasm? How could they be helped to become more dynamic as persons and more interested in doing things?
3. How do I feel about discovering and using the special gift I have been given as a follower of Jesus? In what way could I pool it with the gifts of others in the Body of Christ?

## FORMAT FOR SMALL GROUP SHARING

The material of this book can be used to help busy people put reflection into their lives through the establishment of a reflections group or small christian community. The small group would meet in homes every 2 or 3 weeks for sessions of about 2 hours, following the format indicated below.

To get a group started you only need to look around your church congregation, religious community, or circle of acquaintances for different kinds of people who are desirous of reflecting together on gospel values in their lives. Ideally both men and women of various ages and vocations would come. What may be most critical is to find a time every couple weeks when all would be free. Hold the number to between 8 to 12, so that each may have time to speak when you gather, and yet the group may not get too small should several not be able to attend at a given session.

Once a group begins it is strongly recommended that no new members be added to the group for the duration of the material in this book, and that no occasional visitors would be invited to a group session. It takes time to grow in trust as a group. We are called upon to love these given people as the members of a small community. To get a group going with the members really committed to one another is no small achievement. When any new member is admitted the whole life of the group changes in the sense of needing to start all over again on the trust level.

Before arriving for the session, each member is responsible to read and ponder the material in the

appointed chapter of the book, including the scripture references and the questions for reflection. This
material begins with the chapter entitled *His Mother*.
Although a whole chapter could be used for a given
session, groups may find it more satisfactory to spend
two or three sessions on each chapter, selecting for
each session a different scripture passage for reflection and a different question for dialogue.

Each session needs a *facilitator*. The group may
decide to ask two people to act as co-facilitators. The
facilitator(s) can be the same for many sessions, or the
group members may prefer to take turns facilitating,
perhaps on the basis of whose home hosts the session.

The facilitator's job is mainly to *keep the schedule,*
by getting the session started and having people pay
attention to the time allotted for each section. Some
silence is to be expected and should not be cause for
nervousness or embarrassment. Such silence can aid
reflection and be a sign of friendship.

## GETTING RE-ACQUAINTED TIME (15 minutes)

This period of time sets a tone of friendliness and
informality. When a small group comes together for
prayer or dialogue it is important to know what the
members bring with them to the gathering. This time
of sharing is not to be used as a waiting period until
all members have arrived. It begins only when all are
ready for the session to start. *Individuals are invited
to say how they have been feeling and what has been
happening in their lives since the last session.*

## *SHARING SCRIPTURE* (15 minutes)

The facilitator begins this section by *reading aloud the scripture passage* selected from the *Passages for Reflections* at the end of the chapter. Hopefully each member will bring a copy of the Bible, or at least of the New Testament, so all can easily follow along.

After a period of silent reflection, anyone begins the sharing by saying what this passage, or some of its details, mean to him or her. This is not a time to ask questions about the passage. It is a time of listening to the heart and sharing what the scripture says to one's own life situation.

## *DIALOGUE* (45 minutes)

The facilitator begins this section by *reading a question* from the *Questions for Dialogue* at the end of the chapter. Dialogue is not simply discussion of an idea, but involves reflection on *life experience.* We may not agree with what another says; however, by listening to one another with the heart we come to a much greater understanding of what is behind the words of the other.

When a person shares his or her insight, opinion, conviction or experience, this is a gift of the person to the others. It is to be received with gratitude as something shared from the heart. It may not be the person's last word on the subject, but is offered as of possible benefit to the others. Though no one is forced to share, the group will want to draw all its members into the experience of giving and receiving as they search together for God's truth. The Lord gifts us with one another and wishes the light and love he has placed in each heart to be shared with the others.

## *SHARING PRAYER* (10 minutes)

This section is begun by the facilitator *re-reading the scripture passage* which was used in the section on Sharing Scripture. After some silence, individuals pray out loud in respose to the passage and to what has been shared during the session. Don't say, "I want to pray that . . . ", but address God in your own words, such as, "Father, . . . " or "Lord Jesus, . . . " At this time the only words spoken are addressed to God. There is no discussion with one another. The period of prayer is ended by reciting a prayer in common, such as the Our Father.

## *EVALUATION OF THE SESSION* (5 minutes)

The facilitator invites each person to say *how this session was beneficial and/or disappointing.* There is no response after each person's sharing. Being faithful to this evaluation time will encourage people to continue in the small group rather than drop out when they feel their needs or expectations are not being heard. The facilitator ends this section by announcing the material to be prepared for the next session.

*SOCIAL TIME* (30 minutes)

The social time is no less important than any other part of the session for achieving the purposes of the small group. If a refreshment is served, it should be nothing more elaborate than coffee, tea, and cookies. This avoids "dessert contests", and enables those with little or no income to have the group meet at their home. Occasionally some kind of CREATIVE RECREATION may be planned. What is most important in the social time is the opportunity to be friends and to talk about whatever one wishes.

# Diagrams

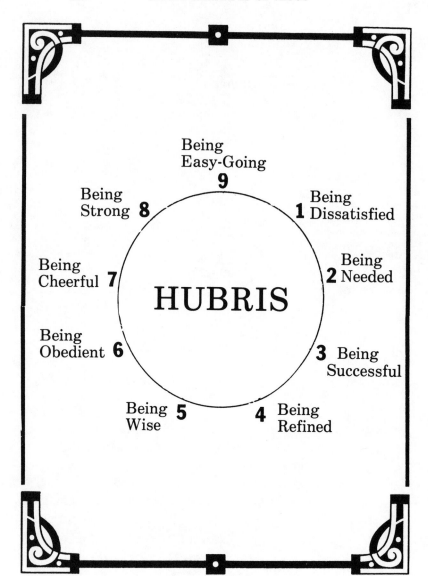

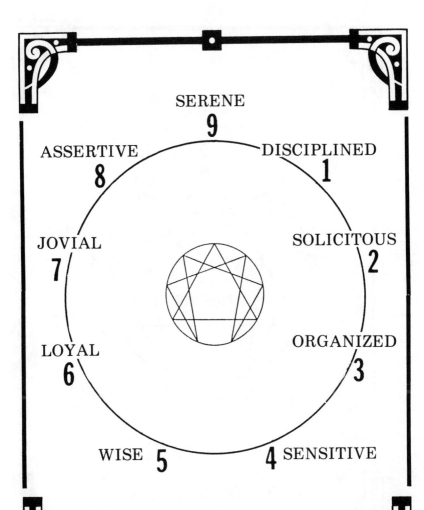

SERENE
9

ASSERTIVE
8

DISCIPLINED
1

JOVIAL
7

SOLICITOUS
2

LOYAL
6

ORGANIZED
3

WISE 5

4 SENSITIVE

THE NINE PORTRAITS of JESUS

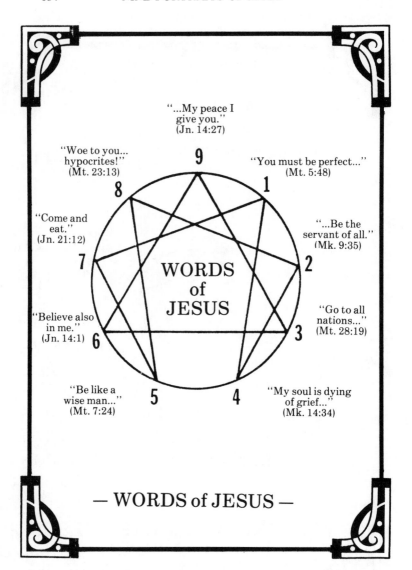

"...My peace I give you."
(Jn. 14:27)

"Woe to you... hypocrites!"
(Mt. 23:13)

"You must be perfect..."
(Mt. 5:48)

"Come and eat."
(Jn. 21:12)

"...Be the servant of all."
(Mk. 9:35)

WORDS of JESUS

"Go to all nations..."
(Mt. 28:19)

"Believe also in me."
(Jn. 14:1)

"Be like a wise man..."
(Mt. 7:24)

"My soul is dying of grief..."
(Mk. 14:34)

9   8   1   7   2   6   3   5   4

— WORDS of JESUS —